Under My Wings

My Life as an Impresario

Under My Wings

MY LIFE AS AN IMPRESARIO

Paul Szilard

As Told to Howard Kaplan

LIMELIGHT EDITIONS
New York

First Edition   January 2002

Published by Proscenium Publishers Inc., 118 East 30th Street, New York, NY 10016.

Manufactured in the United States of America.

Library of Congress Cataloging-in-Publication Data

Szilard, Paul, 1912–
  Under my wings : my life as an impresario / Paul Szilard, as told to Howard Kaplan.
     p. cm.
  ISBN 0-87910-964-5
  1. Szilard, Paul, 1912– 2. Impresarios—Hungary—Biography.
3. Ballet—History—20th century. I. Kaplan, Howard, 1960– II. Title.
  GV1785.S95 A3 2001
  792.8'092—dc21

Library of Congress Control Number: 2001050212

Designed by Mulberry Tree Press, Inc. (www.mulberrytreepress.com)

For my sister Martha
and my wife Ariane

CONTENTS

ACKNOWLEDGMENTS

GRATEFUL ACKNOWLEDGMENTS to my co-author, Howard Kaplan, my publisher, Melvyn Zerman, my assistant, Paul Lucas, my editor, Mark N. Grant, my wife Ariane, and also to Robert Tracy, Oleg Briansky, Clive Barnes, Judith Jamison, Ann Barzel, and Michael Kidd for their help in making this book a reality.

And special thanks to my first teacher—V. G. Troyanoff—who made me a dancer.

—*Paul Szilard*
New York City
April 2001

INTRODUCTION

*T*HERE IS SOMETHING ABOUT THE PROFESSION of impresario, the entire tribe of them, that has fascinated me ever since I learned that such weird and exotic beings existed. I think I originally imagined them looking a little like Serge Diaghilev—imperious and immaculate, pleasingly plump, a haughty look perhaps accentuated by a monocle, a large black coat, impeccably draped and preferably with an astrakhan collar, and possibly a cigar, about which its provenance as Havana it would not occur to anyone to question. A grandee of café society, yet a man of classless class, who wore his cultural and intellectual distinction as casually as a subtle aroma of cologne.

Of course, when I actually began to meet these impresario creatures, I did discover that my earlier imaginings were a little less than precise. Heaven's central casting did not invariably provide the perfect type—and just as I discovered to my regret that all critics did not look all that much like George Sanders in *All About Eve*, so all impresarios did not look all that much like Léon Bakst's portrait of Serge Diaghilev. Yet it didn't matter. In my eyes they were still magic creatures, men and women who—in the theater or the concert hall—enabled art to happen.

It's a strange profession, isn't it? Not an artist, yet hopefully with an artist's taste, not even a critic, yet certainly with a critic's judgment. Indeed an impresario is a critic who puts his money where his opinion is, a man making his living not so much off the artist but through the artist. A man who presents, but first has to choose; a man who encourages, but first has to discern; a man who spreads a message that he first has to receive. And also a man who lives dangerously not only on his own wits, but on the wit of others. To some extent, like a critic, he is a parasite, but, even more than the critic, he has to be symbiotic with his host. He has to help others before he can help himself. And he also lives a hell of an interesting life.

Actually being an impresario, or for that matter a producer, has been a career I have idly but quite often considered for myself—although after every such consideration I reluctantly concluded that I had not the nerve, nerves or organizational skills such a career inevitably demands. Nor, for that matter, would I have the patience or sheer courage. I am more suited to sniping from the sidelines than managing the game—to each his own.

Still I consider it my good fortune that as a critic I have had the opportunity to study quite a number of impresarios from close quarters, and, finding some of them fascinating, have been on occasion unwise enough to become friends with them. Unwise? Yes, in quite a profound way. Critics and impresarios make odd couples. You never agree all the time with anyone—kith, kin, lovers or close friends—and a disagreement between an impresario and a critic will almost certainly carry with it certain financial implications, as well as that special sense of betrayal we all feel when a friend disagrees with that very personal thing, our own artistic taste and judgment. The late Sol Hurok, a man I was proud to count as a friend, and from whom I learned a lot of horse sense about the performing arts, once told me: "You know, Clive, the critic's job is to sell tickets." I replied: "Sol, you are absolutely right, but we get to choose the tickets we feel are worth selling." You can immediately see the difficulty and the potential pitfalls and pratfalls.

Sol, like many impresarios, was a colorful, larger than life personality, a generous spirit (yes, he could also be mean, but the spirit was willing) and a fund of stories, a few unlikely, and all starring himself as hero. At the end of his life—and we had our last lunch together a day or so before he died—he tended towards garrulity, telling the same stories over and over. I never had the unkindness to point this boring fact out, hoping perhaps that when I too am reduced to the same geriatric infirmity no one will have the unkindness to point it out to me—so possibly I was half-unconsciously paying dues towards such life insurance. And after all, I owed him hours and hours of pleasure.

There have been two other impresarios I have been particularly drawn to—one was Julian Braunsweg, not all that well-known, but the founder with Alicia Markova and Anton Dolin of London Festival Ballet, and, of course, the irrepressible hero of these memoirs, Paul Szilard. First something on Braunsweg. I suppose almost every impresario has to have something of the rogue in his personality— they are after all in part kidders and conjurors—but Braunsweg gave the indefinable but pungent impression that he had rather more than was strictly necessary. Yet he lost a fortune pouring his own money—and that of his long-suffering but intensely loyal wife—into the limitless needs of running a then totally unsubsidized ballet company, in the bizarre hope that one day he and it would strike it rich. Yet, I must say, Julian lived quite well—presumably on credit, expense accounts and income tax deductions. His accountant—whom I also knew slightly—was heroic.

Yet of all three of these impresarios, unquestionably my favorite is Paul. Read these quixotic memoirs, a picaresque journey through late 20th century dance, and you'll soon see why. I don't quite remember when I met him—it's lost in the midst of those mists of antiquity—but I was always drawn to his unusual character, a wonderful mix of blunt honesty, bitchy wit and oddly self-deprecating charm. Perhaps it was also because he's Hungarian, and I myself have more than enough Hungarian blood in me for my DNA to dance continually a sort of Jewish czárdás. I have never really believed there was anything in this kind of racial profiling, but I must admit I always seem to get on with Hungarians suspiciously well. And when I first went there, Budapest appeared a lot like home.

Paul has had a wonderful life—and it shows. I've never been able to quite pin him down on anything, and I've been careful never to let him pin me down on anything either. I guess it's the Hungarian connection. But his stories are a delight, and his opinions, although often impossible, are trenchant and always amusing. Of course, I thank God, Terpsichore, or both that Paul never became a critic. His private opinions—never publicly expressed— would devastate whole areas of international dance. Yet when he likes something, his enthusiasm can light up the sky. Also—and this is unusual—what he likes and dislikes often has a cheering lack of relationship with what he is actually himself promoting. And because he soon realized that being as stubborn as a log I was not subject to influence, happily he never spares me his highly opinionated opinions. And interestingly when we disagree—even on the touchy subject of dance or dancers he is himself promoting—he appears to worry about it as little as I do. Another Hungarian connection, I suspect.

Although I've known Paul a long time—about thirty-five years I suppose—a lot of this book came completely fresh to me. Some of its raucous outrageousness hardly surprised me—I think I liked in this context his portrait sketch of a mutual and much-admired friend, Lincoln Kirstein, particularly relishing the anecdote of the steambaths—but there was so much in his story that was new to me. I never saw him dance—although my first sight of him was during the late fifties in a photograph of him near-naked partnering a near-naked Nora Kaye which we ran in a British magazine I was then editing, *Dance and Dancers*. But I have watched him operate so effectively in the wings as manager/impresario. And now storyteller.

And what stories! Who would have guessed that he once auditioned for Lichine—well, that much you might have guessed—but with Georg Solti as his piano accompanist? Then look again at the character studies here—the slightly dubious homophobia of a nose-twitching Balanchine, the supreme self-assurance of Patrick Dupond, the charming slipperiness of Lucia Chase, Erik Bruhn's angst-promoting quest for perfection, the heartfelt agonies, troubles and genius of Alvin Ailey, these and so many more are caught on the wings, sometimes in almost casual sketches, at other times, notably with Ailey, in carefully etched portraits. Note too the picture Paul gives of that chaotic Europe at the turn of the forties, a Europe almost but not quite totally engulfed by war, and certainly not hospitable to a Hungarian passport. By the way, do you really think it's always possible to transfer a rubber stamping on a passport by means of a hard-boiled egg? One day I mean to experiment with it.

Yet what emerges most of all from these sweetly indiscreet memoirs is the portrait of Paul, and rather more shadowy but distinctly omnipresent, his wife, Ariane. Paul himself comes across as the india-rubber optimist, the fierce, indomitable survivor, that clearly all impresarios need to be. His entire career has provided the template for his entire career. It is all one piece, such as his running around from country to country, from dance studio to dance studio, from Paris's Salle Wacker to London's West Street—who would have imagined he took classes with Vera Volkova and the adorable little Stanislas Idzikowsky (and yes, Stas could turn like a top right into his seventies) in London? But all his adventures in Europe and the Orient, from managing the rich and eccentric Anna Galina's troupe to taking American Ballet Theatre to Europe, or, back in America, persuading Alicia Alonso and three other temperamental diva-ballerinas to behave themselves in a performance of *Pas de Quatre*, are part of the fabric of his whole life in dance. Over the years Paul has gotten to go everywhere—nowadays it's Concorde to Europe but earlier travel came in humbler packages—and knows everyone, and, of course, everyone's gossip.

Naturally Paul being Paul he tells all he knows—gossip to Paul is mother's milk. Yet in this book, Paul is never unkind. What I personally like most about the man is his unexpectedly diffident generosity of spirit. He giggles at life, he giggles at himself, but he has this down-to-earth understanding of what it means to live, work and survive, and those giggles are never petty. They indicate, as Shakespeare said, "What fools these mortals be." So his wickedest story has the sting of compassion in his tale.

But if Paul is compassionate he is also extraordinarily shrewd— he is nobody's fool, not even his own. He seems that rare creature—and read these memoirs bearing this in mind—who really has no hypocrisy in his make-up and disapproves of it in others, as well as pomposity and pretentiousness. Yet you rarely find him judgmental—he passes off the world's faults with a laugh rather than a sneer or frown, and he is as open about his own peccadilloes as he is free with other people's.

I always forget how old Paul is—he makes no secret of it, finding it rather a subject of personal pride, but I have no head for numbers—but he is enormously young for his age. His secret, and it's hardly a secret, is his enthusiasm, which bubbles like that of a teenager. His eyes are constantly glinting, brightly searching for the new and unexpected—and I think you will find that search providing the thread which runs through this book. He leaves the impression of being one who has liked what he has found, but is still searching. He's not old because he's still restless, and old people are not restless, they're resting. So, if I were to be asked to offer a subtitle for these memoirs, I think I would suggest: "The Happy Story of a Restless Man." And it is a story that is evidently and cheerfully continuing. Why not?

—*Clive Barnes*

FOREWORD

I LOVE PAUL BECAUSE HE'S DONE SO MUCH for the Alvin Ailey American Dance Theater, as well as for me personally. He's been impresario of the company for more than thirty years, and helped to bring Alvin's message to the world. Early on, when we were a small company, he booked us into venues where no one else had put us before. But Paul had large plans for us and he believed in Alvin and Alvin's vision. We took a step up with Paul, and we're still stepping up, thanks to him.

Paul was instrumental in propelling my career in very interesting ways. In the early 1970s, after Alvin choreographed *Cry* for me, Paul asked me to appear as a guest artist in many of the galas he was putting together. Those were wonderful evenings when dancers from around the world would perform on the same stage. Both Alvin and Paul were responsible for my doing a modern dance during those classical galas. There I was, a five-foot-ten black woman, with short hair and a long skirt, dancing to taped music. Everybody else performed with a string orchestra, and wore tutus and classical ballet costumes. But *Cry* brought down the house every evening. I think it acted as release for the audience.

After that, my career rocketed forward, and Paul paired me with people that I don't think anybody else would have thought of. Paul arranged for me to dance with Mikhail Baryshnikov in Alvin's *Pas de Duke*. Who else would have thought of that? When John Neumeier told Paul that he was choreographing *Josephslegende*, Paul told him, "I have the perfect person for you." That opportunity to dance the role of Potiphar's Wife at the Vienna State Opera was a tremendous gift to me from Paul—a treasure. And Paul also had something to do with where I sit today. He suggested to Alvin that I eventually succeed him as Artistic Director of the Ailey company, though it was up to Alvin to make that choice.

Paul has had so much to do with creating arenas for other people to shine in. For me, that's his greatest accomplishment—allowing so many artists not just to be seen worldwide, but to thrive. He's also very colorful and very loving, with a heart of gold. Plus, he has the most cutting sense of humor of anyone I know, and he's able to get away with it, because there's no one else quite like him. He has boundless energy and enthusiasm and I hope he never runs out of steam.

I'm delighted that Paul has written his memoirs and is sharing his stories of life and dance. With *Under My Wings*, everyone can read what an extraordinary life he's led.

—*Judith Jamison*

PREFACE

*M*EN, NOT ONLY CATS, CAN HAVE NINE LIVES and Paul Szilard has had nine times that many. A dancer, teacher, and an impresario, he has had an amazingly rich life, running the gamut from heartbreaks and brushes with death to triumphs and celebrations.

A friend to many, he has known, helped, loved, and admired the most important artists of the last century (in all disciplines), and this funny and moving book presents a rich portrait of the arts in the twentieth century.

A wonderful storyteller and a keen observer of human behavior, he is able to make those of us who were there remember events as though they happened yesterday, and those who were not wish that they were.

When the first Academy Award is presented for a life well and fully lived, Paul Szilard will be the recipient.

—Violette Verdy

Under My Wings

MY LIFE AS AN IMPRESARIO

PART I

HUNGARIAN PASSPORT

Buda and Pest

*B*UDAPEST IS A VERY OLD AND BEAUTIFUL CITY, divided in two. Buda is hilly and rural, while Pest, where I was born, is cosmopolitan. Pest is filled with architecturally important buildings, and is the district where the arts thrived. It's the home of the Opera House and the National Theater, two institutions that marked my childhood. The royal palace was in Buda, as were the elaborate buildings of the aristocrats that sprung up around the royal residence like stars in a constellation. Also in Buda, the *Màtyàs Templom*, the main church, is a magnificent creation, because Hungary was the first European country to have Catholic kings, and they spared no expense.

My early years were spent in Pest, where we lived in a big apartment building. Actually, it was one of four identical square buildings with a courtyard and a breezeway that caught the wind on warm summer days, funneling it into our apartment through picture windows. We were a close family—my parents, my sister Martha, and me—and were financially comfortable enough to have servants and governesses. These young women came from Germany and we always addressed them as Fraulein. They wore starched white and gray uniforms with skirts that swept the floor as they walked. Martha and I could speak German when we were five years old, even before we could speak Hungarian. Fraulein-this or Fraulein-that wheeled us in our prams to the island of Margit Sziget. There were children there all the time, with governesses that flocked together like sea birds. It's an island in the city, and we lived very close to the bridge that led to Margit

Sziget. In fact, from our windows we could see the Danube, blue and flowing, and just beyond it, Margit Sziget. When we were older, the governesses walked us to school, but I began to be ashamed of them, or ashamed of having to be walked to school, so I begged my Fraulein to let me go the last block by myself. She understood, but if I turned around, she was still there waiting to make sure that I entered the school gates without incident.

It was, I believe, a very good upbringing. We even had a second home in the town of Balaton. We spent our vacations and summers there in a comfortable old house by the lake. My father was a stockbroker and we lived a typical middle-class life in Hungary. When Hitler occupied the country, all that began to change. My parents were separated and my mother was placed in a concentration camp. But they were lucky, and survived. After the war, they managed to get to Switzerland and stayed with my wife's family for more than a year before I was able to bring them to the United States. All in all, I don't think my parents had a very happy marriage, but they stayed together to keep the family whole.

My parents were opposite in many ways. My father was traditional and conservative, while my mother was open-minded and curious. He died at eighty-six in New York City, and my mother died at the age of ninety-two and a half. Though she lived with my sister in Texas, she loved to visit me in New York and go to the theater and fine restaurants. She carried herself very elegantly, walked with a shiny black cane, and smoked like a chimney till the last day of her life. She knew how I lived and what I did, even in my private life. Unlike my disapproving father, however, she wanted to know *all* the details.

Our parents saw to it that Martha and I had a good, firm education. At the gymnasium we studied all the academic classes, including Latin, from the minute we walked through the door until the time of our graduation. I chose to study French there, too, which gave me an advantage when learning the terms of classical ballet. They also saw to it that we attended performances like the National Theater's vivid productions of Shakespeare. After school we had private lessons at home. There was very little time for loafing around.

Martha studied piano and voice and was a very good singer. I, too, was quite musical and studied piano with Karola Bartók, a relative of one of my favorite composers, Béla Bartók, whom I met a few times. He was elegant and handsome, but quiet and reserved. Despite my lessons with Karola, I began to be more interested in linking movement with music. I gravitated toward the dance.

My best friend, János Hajdu, who became a concert pianist, and I would get together after school or on the weekends and listen to music. He'd play the piano for hours, and would explain the music to me. We also had discussions about the arts and the important artists of the day. I find it funny now when I see young people walk in a group and each one is listening to his own set of headphones, tuned out from the immediate world around them. János was as close to me as a brother. He helped to open my eyes (and ears) to classical music. He became a very important concert artist, but died during the war, in a concentration camp. He was Jewish.

I went to the opera and the ballet all the time, and soon I began to study dance with V. G. Troyanoff, who had the best school in Budapest. I first met Troyanoff one August, when I was waiting tables at a summer hotel. After watching me balance trays for a couple of weeks while remaining relatively calm, he approached me and told me that I had a very good physique for dancing and that I should give serious thought to becoming a classical dancer. I couldn't believe that somebody was speaking the exact words I had wanted to hear. I had long imagined myself cut from the same cloth as a dancer, but Troyanoff was the first professional to look at me and think that I had something. After meeting with him a few times, he thought he "could make a dancer out of me." I was amazed. It was what I had always wanted, so when he asked me if I'd like to be a dancer, I said yes, and agreed to work with him. He instructed me to come to his studio in Budapest when the summer was over.

I remember how much I looked forward to going to the studio. When I arrived, I was overwhelmed. Troyanoff called me into a grand, mirrored room, and asked me to do a few things at the barre so he could have a good look at my feet, my extensions, and my general carriage. That was about all that could be expected of me, because I had never taken a ballet class. He was kind about my abilities, but his interest in me was not based solely on my potential. It was also based on it being so rare in those days to find a young man interested in the dance at all that he didn't want to miss out on the opportunity.

I didn't quite know how to tell my parents the "good" news. Though both were interested in the arts, it was taboo for a boy to express interest in the dance, let alone make the commitment I was prepared to make. My parents tried to persuade me otherwise and got me an office job which I kept for two days. I hated it so much, and made such grievous errors, that I was thrown out even before my pencils needed to be resharpened. So I went to Troyanoff and told him that I could not afford to take classes. He agreed to teach me for free, in exchange for my working in the school's office, where I helped to register new pupils and did other secretarial odds and ends.

So, I went back, and said nothing to my parents. My father was a stockbroker and expected me to follow in his footsteps, but I wouldn't hear of it. After beginning my work with Troyanoff, my father arranged another job for me, but I couldn't take it because it would have interfered with my ballet classes. I had a very wealthy aunt who used to give me some pocket money every time I went to see her. She and her husband owned a specialty food shop. Though she was rather unsophisticated and had no idea about art, she was down-to-earth and practical, and loved me very much. She was my only hope.

One day I went to see her, and over a cup of strong tea I confessed everything to her. She sat, very upright, and smiled when I told her about my ballet classes. I told her that I wanted more than anything to be a ballet dancer, but I needed her help. She placed her china cup back in its saucer, pressed a perfectly ironed napkin to her lips, and told me she would help. With the money she gave me, plus the money I made working for Troyanoff, I was able to get by.

As my studies continued, I began to do all kinds of dancing with his group, including Spanish dancing. Though I started late, I had a very flexible body. I was thin and had good, quick feet.

One afternoon, Tamara Karsavina, former ballerina of the Maryinsky Theater and the Diaghilev Ballets Russes, came to visit the school. The doors to the studio opened, and in walked this elegant woman. She was striking. All the students were speechless. She was one of the most renowned dancers in the world. Her entourage included Tamara Nijinsky, Vaslav's daughter, who was very young at the time. Karsavina was married to Lord Henry J. Bruce, the English ambassador to Hungary, and was friends with the great dramatic actress Emilia Markus, the mother-in-law of Nijinsky. And, of course, Karsavina had been Vaslav Nijinsky's outstanding partner.

The women sat quietly throughout the class, while we did our exercises at the barre and in the center of the studio. As we were filing out, Karsavina stopped me, placed her gloved hand on my shoulder, and said, "Well done, young man. One of these days you will be a very good dancer." I held onto her words for years. They helped me get through some difficult times.

In addition to taking class, I tried to see every dance performance or concert that I could. I heard Rachmaninoff and child prodigy Yehudi Menuhin. Even when I had no money, I managed to sneak into the theater, and, for the most part, was not caught. Sometimes, the theater director would let you be an extra, and it was terribly exciting to be on stage in the opera, even if all you got to do was cross the stage with a lit torch. Once, I appeared as a cardinal in *Tosca*. I didn't speak or sing a word, but to this day I still remember the power I felt onstage when I was dressed in a long, velvet robe, carrying a cross that was bigger than I was. I was so proud to be the star of the evening just walking across the stage!

I was never interested in any kind of sport, only the arts, though my parents forced me into ice skating, which I hated. I think they wanted to air me out once in a while. I attended drama school, because in order to be a good dancer, you also had to be a good actor. We had to attend performances at the National Theater. I saw Shakespeare repertory in Hungarian that had been translated by a very prominent writer named Madács, who was a political prisoner and had been locked away in jail for many years. That's where he did his writing. They said his translations were so wonderful that the plays sounded better in Hungarian than in English.

There came a time when my mother thought I should know more about art if I was to succeed as an artist, and my parents paid for me to travel throughout Italy. I went to most of the big cities and visited all the museums and churches that I possibly could. I think that one, huge dose of art was enough for a lifetime. At the time, I couldn't help think: one more painting of a Pope sitting in a chair and I'll go nuts . . . . Today, I much prefer to go to museums for modern art, like MOMA in New York. I feel much more related to the modern, twentieth century sensibility, than I do to the paintings and landscapes of another time. Maybe that's because all that was taken away from me when World War II broke out.

I left Hungary not long after I finished my *matura* and graduated from the gymnasium (college). In 1938, I went with Troyanoff and his small company to Sweden, where we were engaged to perform. And though I had the leading roles in Troyanoff's ballets, I began to feel that I had no future in the company. In effect, I had done all I could with his group. I told Troyanoff that I had no intention of returning to Hungary. If I went back home, I'd be drafted into the military. The war was imminent, and I didn't know what I was going to do. I decided to go to Paris and continue my studies.

Paris, the Studio Wacker (La Salle Wacker), and Violette Verdy

I had an uncle on my mother's side who lived in Paris. He ran a laundry shop, and had an apartment above it. He liked me very much and paid for my living expenses, including my hotel—a crummy little room on the Rue Jacob.

The Studio Wacker, the center of the dance, was in a very old building in the Place de Clichy. For dancers, it was more important than the Louvre. They sought it out like Lourdes. I never had enough money when I was in Paris, so I got free lessons because teachers liked me. I still owe Madame Rousanne Sarkissian to this day! And when you finished her class, you were expected to pay immediately. Madame would move two chairs to the entrance of the studio. On one she'd place an old, cracked soup plate, and on the other, herself. When you left class, you were to say goodbye to Madame and place your francs in the plate. Madame Rousanne noticed everything. If somebody walked out without paying, Madame would stop them and ask for her money. When I had money, I put it in the plate. More often than not, the dancers would pay her when they got work.

All the greatest dancers passed through the doors of the Wacker at some point in their careers, because all the great teachers were there, including my main teachers, Preobrajenska, and Madame Rousanne, who also taught Maurice Béjart, Zizi Jeanmaire, Mireille Briansky, Violette Verdy, Lycette Darsonval, and many of the leading dancers of the Paris Opera Ballet. (Serge Peretti, star of the Paris Opera, would often do the barre on toe in toe shoes.)

As a matter of fact, when I was taking class, Violette Verdy used to stand behind me at the barre. By the time she was eleven years old, she was already an extraordinary technician. Today, she's best known for her work with Ballets de Paris de Roland Petit, American Ballet Theatre, and New York City Ballet (which she joined as a principal in 1958). She had a flexibility in her feet which was unusual, plus a musicality that made all the other students look at her, even when she was standing still. As a young girl, she had studied piano and violin, and you could feel that musical upbringing every time she moved. She carried that with her all her life, so that when she became a leading dancer, her musicality separated her from other dancers. I always felt that a dancer who danced music should know music.

Through the years, I became close friends with Violette, as well as with her mother, who was a real "ballet mother." She was constantly watching Violette's every move, and Violette couldn't take a step without her permission. Her mother was her mentor, cook, doctor, agent, and advisor all in one. She helped her in so many ways, but I also felt that Violette was hurt by this because she did not have any freedom.

When Violette was eleven years old, Roland Petit engaged her in his company, Les Ballets des Champs-Élysées, which, at the time, was under the management of Sol Hurok. When leading dancer Colette Marchand injured herself, Hurok advised Petit to let Violette step in and dance *Carmen*. Violette had a great success in that ballet, and her reputation just escalated after that.

Shortly after, Roland decided to put Violette in his signature ballet, *Le Loup*, and she was an overnight sensation. In 1954, she got a telephone call from the Hurok office, and they asked her to join the London Festival Ballet and dance with English dancer John Gilpin, who later became artistic director and principal dancer of the company. They danced together in *The Nutcracker*. Ann Barzel, the dance critic from Chicago, filmed the performance and later on showed the film to Nora Kaye. When Nora saw it she said, "My God, this girl should join ABT." That became the start of Violette's career with American Ballet Theatre.

For ABT, Violette created the title role in the ballet *Miss Julie*, dancing with Erik Bruhn. This was an amazing ballet choreographed by Swedish dancer and choreographer Birgit Cullberg, based on the play of the same name by August Strindberg. Once I saw her performance I said to Violette, "I think that you should join the New York City Ballet. Let me handle that." She agreed, so I took George Balanchine and Lincoln Kirstein to a performance, though I heard that they very seldom went to ABT. Once they saw Violette, they decided to engage her. Mr. B always liked France and French dancers. I negotiated her contract, and she stayed with New York City Ballet for eighteen years. Violette married the son of Lord Kenneth Clark, Colin Clark. Colin's twin sister, Colette, was working with Margot Fonteyn at the time and said to Violette, "You've got to meet my brother. He's a bum, but a very charming bum." Apparently, she fell for the bum, and married him. I was in New York at the time, but traveled to London for the wedding, along with New York City Ballet dancers Patricia Wilde and John Taras. It was an extraordinary social event attended by Margot Fonteyn, Vivien Leigh, and Marie Rambert, among others. Pierre Cardin designed her wedding dress, and she looked beautiful. The wedding took place at Lord Clark's castle, Saltwood Castle, which was filled with paintings by El Greco and Delacroix and sculptures by Henry Moore. Unfortunately, the marriage did not last very long.

I continued to handle all of Violette's contracts when she became director of the Paris Opera Ballet, and then the Boston Ballet. Now she's a guest teacher all around the world. She recently told me, "I am so happy that you are looking after me, because finally I can fly business class, rather than economy."

At the Studio Wacker, I divided my time between Madame Rousanne and Olga Preobrajenska, who became known as the teacher of Margot Fonteyn. One day, I decided that I wanted to film Preobrajenska's class, with her permission. She had never let anyone record her class. I had no sense of filming or mechanics. Unfortunately, I did not develop the film right away, and, years later, took the camera with me on tour with New York City Ballet to Japan. I began to take pictures of Melissa Hayden from the wings. When the film was finally developed it was double-exposed: Preobrajenska and Melissa were running at each other in what must have been the strangest partnering between two dancers that I have ever brought together!

Within a few months, I met Aubrey Hitchins, who had been one of the partners of Anna Pavlova. He was the ballet master of the Opéra-Comique in Paris and engaged me as soloist. We performed at a festival in the city of Caen, at the opera house where Bizet's opera *Carmen* was given, in celebration of the opera's anniversary. Aubrey was very tall and thin. Grotesque, actually. We always made jokes about him. One day he got mad at us because he was dancing the "Habanera" from *Carmen* and it just looked ridiculous. I told Aubrey's boyfriend that Aubrey looked like somebody had slammed a door in his face. He repeated it to Aubrey and I almost lost my job.

Au Revoir

After leaving Troyanoff, I went back and forth between Paris and London. With very little money, I crossed the channel to England, and studied with Stanislas Idzikowsky in London. He had been the partner of Olga Preobrajenska at the Maryinsky Theater in Russia. When I took classes with him, he was in his fifties but seemed in his sixties or seventies to me. The London studio was not heated and ice-cold, so Idzikowsky would teach class fully dressed. But he was such a superior technician he could execute eight to ten pirouettes, even in his everyday shoes, like nobody else.

Idzikowsky was pleased with my progress, and suggested that I audition for the Ballets Russes de Monte Carlo who were guesting at Covent Garden. They were embarking on a tour of Australia and were looking for another dancer. Idzikowsky told me he would take me to see David Lichine, ballet master of the Ballets Russes. So one day we attended a performance, and afterwards went backstage to look for Lichine. Soon enough, we found his dressing room, and Idzikowsky knocked on the door. Suddenly, we heard screaming and the sound of something crashing. The door flew open and Lichine's future wife, the great Russian ballerina Tatiana Riabouchinska, one of the three original "baby ballerinas" of the Ballets Russes, ran out of the room, while Lichine threw a toe shoe at her. Idzikowsky turned to me and said, "I don't think this is the right time for me to introduce you."

Without an introduction, I auditioned for Lichine a few days later. I had the help of Antal Doráti, another Hungarian, who was conductor of the Ballets Russes. He told me a young conductor was coming from Budapest to London for the first time. His name was Georg Solti, whom I knew from our early days in Budapest when we were both connected to the Academy of Music. A protégé of Issay Dobrowen, a famous Russian conductor, Solti was invited to conduct one matinee at the Ballets Russes.

Solti and I used to go out every day and walk around London, speaking to each other in Hungarian. Because we both were broke, we used to go to a cafeteria together on the Strand, where you got a slice of bread when you ordered coffee. The ketchup was also free, so we were each able to have a ketchup sandwich. "Georg," I said one day, "I have an audition coming up, and I'm wondering if you'll do me the favor of playing for me? I have no money to hire a pianist."

"Of course," he said, "I'll meet you at Covent Garden."

I had already been giving dance performances of my own, in the style known as *recital de danse*. These were recitals in the style of Harald Kreutzberg and Alexander Sakharoff, where a dancer would present his own choreography, while also being responsible for costumes and music. Connecting movement with feeling was like a concert pianist playing classical music. I became interested in being a concert artist because I was not completely satisfied with classical ballet and the standard repertoire of full-length classics about princes and swans. There was much more room to express myself as an artist in the *recital de danse*.

On the day of the Lichine audition, I arrived at the theater early, went backstage and was told to change. The Ballets Russes was rehearsing, and the iron curtain was down. When I walked out on stage, everybody turned in my direction. I guess I had overdone it a bit, for they looked at me as though I were an alien being and said: "Who the hell is he?" I was wearing my costume for recitals: a long black cape and black tights. Trying to make an impression, I must have looked like Count Dracula. Of course, that wasn't how to dress for an audition, but I didn't know at the time that dancers audition in practice clothes. This was after all the first audition in my life.

David Lichine sat in a chair in front of the iron curtain and yelled, "Are you the one here for the audition?"

"Yes," I said.

"OK, come here. What do you want to do?"

"I have a solo number . . ."

"OK. Do it," he said with a grimace on his face.

I nodded my head to Georg Solti and began to dance the solo I had choreographed to Chopin's *Etudes*, which was a very dramatic and very theatrical piece. Shortly into the first movement, Georg dropped the music and reached down with one hand to find it while he continued to play with the other. It was a disaster. We were not together. It didn't help matters that Lichine was a very nervous director, and was in a very bad mood to boot. He called out, "Stop it. Stop it. Just come here and do these simple steps: glissade assemblé, assemblé, assemblé, entrechat six, entrechat six, glissade assemblé, assemblé, assemblé, entrechat six, entrechat six, pirouette en l'air."

When I completed that he said, "All right, I will let you know."

A couple of days later, Idzikowsky got a message from Lichine, "OK, we will take him." I was ecstatic, but then came the news that because of my wonderful Hungarian passport, I could not get a visa to go to Australia, and the Ballets Russes left without me.

Soon after the Lichine audition, Solti and I said goodbye. We would later see each other in the United States, after the war. In fact, my brother-in-law, Désiré Ligeti, bass-baritone with the San Francisco Opera, arranged for Solti's first conducting performance with the opera. At the opening night party at my sister's house in San Francisco, I brought up our time together at Covent Garden, when he had played for my audition. I thought we would both enjoy a good laugh as I asked him, "Georg, do you remember when you dropped the music during my audition for Lichine, and everything was a mess?"

"No," he answered, "I don't remember." I was shocked. Evidently, he wanted to forget that time when we were broke.

"But Georg," I said, "how will you *ever* conduct if you can't remember?"

He was stunned and changed the subject. Despite his selective memory, Solti did go on to become one of the greatest conductors of the twentieth century. Years later, I accidentally ran into him while strolling in Central Park in New York. He barely muttered "Oh hello Paul" and quickly walked away from me. Though my late brother-in-law Désiré, who had been close to Georg Solti in school in Budapest, had arranged for him to conduct in San Francisco, Solti never returned the favor. He never invited Ligeti, who was a very fine bass-baritone, to sing in Germany after the war.

After the Ballets Russes left without me, I was distraught and went back to my flophouse. I needed some fresh air and climbed up to the roof. On the adjoining roof, a young woman was sitting with her cat, Mooshka. She was a dancer named Ariane Pulver, and we would become friends, partners, and, years later, husband and wife.

Ariane was born in Switzerland and received her degree from the Conservatory of Music in Geneva. She became a professor of music who specialized in teaching piano to children. She also loved dance and played the piano for dance classes. Often, she played for me during rehearsals of ballets that I had choreographed.

In addition to her music, Ariane was a pupil of Émile Jaques-Dalcroze, the Swiss composer and music teacher who originated the movement system known as Eurhythmics. Before that, he had studied with Léo Delibes in Paris and with Anton Bruckner in Vienna. When Dalcroze was a professor at Geneva—he, too, attended the Conservatory of Music—he helped students of music develop a sense of rhythm by translating sounds into physical movements. He was a pioneer of barefoot dancing and employed running, clapping, and rhythm in his system. Dalcroze became one of the most influential teachers in Europe, and taught, among others, Marie Rambert and Hanya Holm.

In Geneva, I watched Dalcroze give a class, and I was fascinated. Eventually, the Dalcroze method became so famous and popular that even Balanchine was interested in it, how movement was connected to music. And certainly, Balanchine was one of the most musical choreographers—ever. In fact, when I first saw Balanchine's *Serenade*, his first ballet in America, I recognized a lot of Dalcroze's influence in the first movement. Balanchine told me that he had a great admiration for Dalcroze. Mr. B and Ariane would talk about Dalcroze whenever they got together. Interestingly, Dalcroze was also a great friend of Igor Stravinsky's, the composer who became Balanchine's frequent collaborator.

Ariane came to be Dalcroze's number one student, and whenever he traveled to another country to teach, she accompanied him to demonstrate. Through Dalcroze, Ariane developed an interest in becoming a dancer herself and traveled to London in 1939, when we met, to join a modern dance group led by Lottie and Ernst Berk.

After a time, Ariane wanted to learn ballet, and she started taking class with me. Though, in my opinion, she had started late for ballet, she was very successful in combining ballet with modern dance and the Dalcroze rhythm. Eventually, we were to do dance recitals in Europe together, where I danced classic ballet, and Ariane, modern.

Later on, when we came to America, Ariane stopped dancing— she finally realized it wasn't her forte. I also think I had something to do with her decision, because I was a very strict teacher and insisted that all my ballet students reach a professional level. I felt Ariane could not be a successful classical dancer because she began her training too late. Her body never really developed the flexibility and pliability that mark a true, classical dancer. When she gave up ballet, she went back to what she did best—teaching piano. She became a professor at the Dalcroze Institute in New York City, on East 73rd Street. The director was Hilda Schuster, who had been a colleague of Ariane's back in Switzerland. Ariane became one of the most popular teachers in the school. Sadly, when Dr. Schuster died, the school closed.

We were in Switzerland when we decided to get married. We'd been living in Geneva with Ariane's parents. We got married in a civil ceremony in Berne, but for Ariane that was not enough. Because she is an extremely devout Catholic, later, in America, she had a French priest marry us in a religious ceremony at a chapel in a brownstone on West 32nd Street, between 9th and 10th Avenues, in Manhattan. Most of the parishioners were Hispanic. I asked my father to be one of the witnesses. He had been annoyed that I lived what he considered a "different" life. Now he was so happy because, he said, finally I'm living a normal life!

During those early days in London, money was always a problem. I managed to get a job as a dancer at the Odeon Cinema. During intermission there was a stage show and I was hired to do an authentic Hungarian dance. All went well till the afternoon I fell on my ass in front of the audience. I was embarrassed, but picked myself up and kept going. The job ended shortly after that. I then began to give private dance classes to a few wealthy women. I still couldn't pay my rent and had to move to a boardinghouse in Lyndon Gardens. The woman who ran the place was quite eccentric and liked to wear long flowery dresses and keep her hair in pigtails. She was a Christian Scientist and didn't believe in medicine or in going to the doctor. Instead, she'd pray.

The minute I walked into her house for the first time, she looked at me and seemed stunned. After we talked a bit, she expressed her belief that I was the reincarnation of an ancient Egyptian deity, and believed the same of herself. She thought that we had been together in another lifetime—probably as a king and a queen—and that our "reunion" was fated. She insisted that I stay at the boardinghouse as a guest and I was of course happy that I didn't have to pay.

One day while I was soaking in the bathtub, she knocked on my door to announce that the immigration officers were downstairs. I threw on some clothes and rushed downstairs to be told that my visa had expired and I had to leave within twenty-four hours. Otherwise I would be put in a detention camp, as Hungarians were now regarded as enemy aliens.

I didn't know what to do and asked Ariane for advice. Her parents were always helping refugees, and she suggested that we go to their home in Switzerland. I had no money for the train, and knew of only one person to whom I could turn for financial help: Lord Howard de Valden. A great fan of the dance, he was an amateur designer and painter, and I had modeled for him quite a few times after meeting him backstage at the Odeon Theater. He lived in a mansion in Belgrave Square where he had a stable converted into an artist's studio. He would send his Rolls-Royce to my flophouse in Lyndon Gardens to pick me up. He was very generous and paid me ten pounds an hour to model wearing a costume of ancient Greece. I remember falling asleep because I was so bored. Even though he was the one painting, he had his teacher with him to look over his shoulder offering corrections.

When Ariane suggested we go to Switzerland, I called Lord de Valden on the telephone and told him what had happened with the immigration officers, and that I had no money. He agreed to help and told me to call his secretary, who in turn told me to come over. When I walked into the house, the secretary asked, "How much do you need?"

"I don't want to tell you how much I need," I said. "You should decide."

He handed me a check for a lot of money, enough to live in Europe for about a year. I packed the few things I had, and Ariane and I crossed the Channel and boarded the last train to Geneva. Shortly after that, Hitler closed the borders.

In Switzerland, Ariane and I decided to become dancing partners. We quickly found a studio in Geneva, and started working with the goal of putting on a joint program. Our friend, Doris Rosio, a well-known concert pianist, was our accompanist. When our program was ready, the three of us went on tour. After Ariane or I danced, Doris would play a solo number. Ariane created contemporary dances with modern music such as Ravel's *Le Tombeau de Couperin*, while I choreographed to classical music by Chopin and Liszt. We also danced some noble Hungarian dances with music by Zoltán Kodály. Ariane and I choreographed a dance where we put ballet and modern together. Since the world was changing, why not reflect those changes in our dance?

After a year, in 1940, the Swiss decided to expel all foreigners. The only remaining free ports from where people could travel to America were in Portugal. But to get to Portugal you had to go through Spain and therefore needed a Spanish visa. We did not know how to get one. It was impossible to get anywhere near the Spanish consulate because hundreds of people were lined up there by five o'clock each morning. And then, at the last minute, Ariane's mother said to me, "Well, I think I have some contacts for you. I believe that I know the consul."

"How do you know him?" I asked.

And then she told me how it all happened.

Many refugees from Franco's Spain and the Spanish Civil War had come to Switzerland, and Ariane's mother heard about a young family of Spanish refugees who were destitute. Ariane's mother wanted to help. She got their address, put together a basket of food, left it on their doorstep, rang the bell, and ran away. She did this each morning for a long time. She would not tell the family who she was, wanting to be mysterious, a bit poetic, and signing a note, "A gift from Rose."

One day, for some reason unknown to us, the young refugee became the Spanish consul in Geneva. When Ariane's mother told me this, I said, "Are you out of your mind? Why haven't you told me this before? I'm sitting here with the possibility of being deported."

Finally, I convinced her to get in touch with him. It was my only hope. So she wrote a letter to the consul and said, "Do you remember Rose? That's me who writes you this letter. I would like to ask you for a favor. Will you help my daughter and her partner to get a visa?" And she explained the mess we were in. The next day, Ariane's mother received an enormous bouquet of flowers from the consul and his family. He wrote a note and said that Ariane and I should come to see him immediately and he'd take care of things. The next day we went to his office, where on the spot he gave me a visa to go to Spain.

The only way out of Switzerland was by train, and none were available since they were all packed with fleeing refugees. Somehow the consul got us two seats on one of the last trains from Geneva to Barcelona.

The following day we boarded the train, which after some hours slowed down and then suddenly stopped when we got to the

Spanish border. There was a problem—and the problem was me. Officers came to our compartment, slid open the heavy wooden and glass doors, and asked everyone for their passports. I was the last one they asked, and I was the one they wanted. I had that wonderful Hungarian passport that branded me an enemy alien. I thought I would be thrown off the train.

I had with me a postcard sent to us from a friend in Spain named Franco. Not *the* Franco, but it was spelled clearly enough on the card for me to make my point.

"Do you see the name on this card?" I asked the officer, showing him the card from my old friend Franco.

He didn't respond.

"Do you know the name Franco?"

"Yes," he said.

"Well, this card is from General Franco, a friend of ours. If you don't let me through, I am going to go to the nearest telephone and call General Franco's office in Spain. The choice is yours."

He got confused, handed back my passport, and let us go on.

In Barcelona, I went to Magrina, the ballet master of the Liceo Opera House. "It's a wonderful occasion that you are here because I would like to take ballet class," he said, and he asked me to give him private ballet lessons. Through Magrina, I began to get other pupils, including the sons and daughters of ambassadors and consuls. My rented studio was slowly filling with the prominent names of Spanish society. Fortunate as this might have been, my goal was to get to America, but the only border open to the West was Portugal. How was I to get a visa to Portugal? A new headache!

One refugee would talk to another refugee, and soon stories spread of how certain people had made their escape. In this way, I heard about a man who was selling phony visas. It was our only way out, and it could have come from the pages of a spy novel. I made contact with him and followed his elaborate instructions. In the middle of the night we went into a seedy café near the water, a smoky gangster café, where we were instructed to meet a man in a black beret. We spotted him across the room, and Ariane and I slowly made our way towards him. We told him that we wanted to get into Portugal. He took a long drag on a cigarette, then said that he could help us. "Meet me here tomorrow," he instructed, "and bring your two passports, and cash, and go to the toilet, then leave your passports and cash in a newspaper on top of the water tank. I will pick up the paper, and return your passports to you the same way, in the toilet stall, in two days."

We really had no idea what to do. But since we were running out of money and out of luck, we had no choice but to follow his instructions, not knowing if we'd ever see our passports again. Ariane and I walked out of the café and barely slept that night, not knowing if we had made a smart or a foolish decision. Unfortunately, this was the only way.

Two days later, I went back to the toilet, and there were our passports, exactly where we had left them two days before. With them were phony visas for Honduras, of all places, which would give us transit visas to enter Portugal. But we were warned: "Never put your foot into Honduras, because you'll be arrested immediately."

As soon as we got into Portugal with my Hungarian passport, we found a cheap pension. Our Swiss money was welcomed. In 1941 it seemed the entire world wanted to go to Portugal, and when you walked out onto the crowded boulevards, it seemed the entire world was there: fallen royalty, like the kings of Romania and Spain, and even Josephine Baker, who had fled from France, were among the displaced. It was so crowded that the police would not let you stay in Lisbon and people were descending upon the provinces.

I had a good friend who was an important newspaper critic. She introduced me to a circle of intellectuals—writers, musicians, artists, and designers—who would get together at a café and spend the night talking about the arts. During that time I met Pedro de Freitas Branco, composer and conductor, who then commanded the center of the Lisbon art world. Through him I met people at the San Carlos Opera House, and I soon started to give class there. One day, I got a message that the Countess of Mafra wanted to meet me to discuss putting together a charity gala at the Opera House to aid the poor. She became my patron. She had been a member of the royal family, but when President Salazar took over Portugal, she lost her position and took the name of Mafra, which was her family's estate. Her wonderful old apartment housed a direct passageway to her box at the Opera House. She had a grand piano in her salon on which the greatest European artists who had performed at her family home, including Artur Rubinstein, Franz Liszt, and Rachmaninoff, had signed their names.

Before we made plans for the charity event, the Countess wanted to generate some publicity for me, but how? She decided that I should give a recital and promptly rented the National Theater, where I presented my evening of *recital de danse*. Marie Levec, concert pianist and wife of Pedro de Freitas Branco, agreed to play for the concert. The Countess called all her once-royal friends and asked, "How many boxes do you want?" She sold out the National Theater in no time. The audience was filled with Portuguese society and my reviews were wonderful, all paving the way for the gala.

I wanted to make a strong impression and chose two ballets for the charity gala. The first was *Sonatina* by Ernesto Halffter, originally composed for La Argentinita. Halffter and I became close friends as we worked together on the ballet, which he conducted. The second ballet on the program was the Schumann *Carnaval*. I followed Fokine's original choreography, changing those parts that I just could not remember. I hired all the dancers, and we had the luxury of several months of rehearsals. One day I was in rehearsal at the opera house when I got a telephone call: "Dr. Schuschnigg would like to talk to you."

That was the last president of Austria, who had escaped to Lisbon and was now a refugee like everybody else. It made little difference what title you held before the war. We were all now living in a city of refugees.

"I have a Jewish pianist who is a fantastic talent who escaped

from Austria with me. Could you use him at the opera house?"
Schuschnigg asked.

"I cannot tell you over the phone. Please send him over and I'll
see."

So he came to the opera, a poor little man who had absolutely
no presence at all.

"Do you know the Schumann *Carnaval*?" I asked him.

He said, "Yes."

"Well, play me a little."

I offered him the music, but he said that he didn't need it. A
concert pianist, he knew the score by heart.

When he started playing, I was amazed! He was tremendously
talented, and I engaged him immediately. Then I introduced him
to the Countess, who liked him from the start, and soon had him
playing in the musical evenings at her salon.

Everything seemed to be going well—until the day the author-
ities told me to get out of Lisbon: my passport had expired! I went
to the Hungarian consulate where, instead of renewing it, they in-
validated it because I refused to return home and serve in the
army. I couldn't get an American visa with an expired passport.
The Hungarian consul was a nasty, awful man who told me that I
had to go back to Hungary and report for military service. When
I told him that I would not return, he took my passport from me
and stamped it *Nem Érvényes Továb* — "not valid any longer."

Now I was in a desperate situation and went to the Countess
for advice. She said, "Paul, I am now going to do something for
you that I would never do for anybody else." She picked up the
telephone and called President Salazar's office, spoke to his secretary and said, "This is the Countess of Mafra, and I would like to
ask the President a great favor." She explained who I was and that
I could not be deported. She talked about the sold-out charity gala
saying, "Please, I must have Mr. Szilard here or the entire evening
will be a failure. We are in the middle of everything. I am asking
the President to help me in this matter."

When she hung up, she said, "Now, we wait." A few days later, a message from the President's office arrived informing her that my visa would be extended.

The charity performance proved to be a success, especially the Schumann *Carnaval*. I was called onto the stage at the San Carlos Opera House to receive one of their highest awards: a miniature, silver boat named for legendary explorer Vasco da Gama. It rested on a red velvet pillow. After that, I was asked to stay and become the ballet master of the Opera House. But my goal was to come to the States, and I felt that it was time to move on. So again I went in search of people who could help me.

I met another colorful Hungarian who was an aristocrat back home but was now an "operator," working out of a café. He offered his assistance. He had a woolly Franz Josef mustache and was at the center of the Hungarian refugee circle. After I told him what had happened to me at the consul's office, he asked to see my passport. He took it from me, then took a fine pen from his breast pocket and wrote the words, "extended for three years" on the passport. I thought this was a surefire way to get me thrown into jail. When I was about to question him, he held up an index finger, as if to say wait a minute. He asked the waitress for a hardboiled egg, and when she returned with one, he peeled it, then rolled the egg on the Hungarian validation I had on a previous page, then rolled the egg back onto my passport. The stamp was reproduced intact. I couldn't believe my eyes. Then he forged the consul's signature. He wiped his hands with a napkin, put his pen back in his pocket, and handed me my passport. All in a day's work for an exiled Count.

It was time to leave Lisbon, but how were we going to get out? We still had our false visas to Honduras, and could secure transit visas that would get us to the United States but would not permit us to stay. I could also never go to Honduras, which didn't seem too troubling at the time. We had to line up at the U.S. consulate with thousands of other refugees. People were given numbers and were told to return in three or four weeks. But the consul knew me and gave me a transit visa to America. And with this I could book passage on a ship.

Finally, after spending a lot of time and money (much of it under the table), we got two tickets on a cargo boat named NIASA that had enough space for 500 people. In fact, there were 5,000 refugees on the boat to make the crossing to the States. We had no bed to sleep on. Ariane slept in a lifeboat that hung over the side of the ship.

It was wartime, and there was a blackout. German U-boats were everywhere. The captain found me one day and said, "Listen, if you will put together some entertainment for the benefit of the sailors, I will arrange for you to have a better place to sleep." That turned out to be on a mattress under a table in the dining room, but it was much better than what we had. I was grateful.

There were two other artists on the boat, Miklos Schwalb, a famous Hungarian pianist, and Jean-Pierre Aumont, the French movie actor. Aumont was very young and very beautiful and traveled with his "friend," who was an ambassador to a Latin American country. They shared the only cabin, and we were all very jealous of that luxury. Despite the difficulties of trying to put a show together on the ship, the three of us managed to pull it off. First I danced, while Schwalb accompanied me on the piano, and then to finish Aumont recited poetry. After that, we collected money for the sailors. Since most of the refugees had some money on them, we were able to present the crew with a fair amount of cash.

We traveled for fifteen days and were never told where we were. There was a blackout most of the time for fear of being attacked by a German U-boat. To our surprise, we landed first in Morocco, though everybody thought we had arrived in America, and it took us another two weeks to sail on to the United States. Immediately when we arrived in New York Harbor, we were taken to Ellis Island. Everyone on board cheered when we passed the Statue of Liberty and we knew that at last we were in the land of freedom. We stayed on Ellis Island for two weeks, along with silent film star Pola Negri, and I have to say now that while it was heaven compared to what we had been through, in many ways it was like a jail. Ariane, being Swiss, was not required to stay on

Ellis Island, but she insisted on remaining with me. When friends of hers heard we were there and came to rescue her, she refused to leave without me. A group of rather starchy looking ladies in long gray skirts and high collars made it their business to act as chaperones for young women who left Ellis Island on their own. When they learned Ariane was Swiss and unmarried, they too tried to convince her to leave Ellis Island, and allow them to take care of her. Ariane took one look at them and said, "Absolutely not. I'd rather go to jail." She was allowed to stay with me.

Men and women slept in separate dormitories, but during the day, we were allowed to mix in a huge day room. There, each person tried to map out a little territory for himself by piling suitcases between his bed and the next. I'll never forget the sound of children screaming and running through the cavernous room. Cooped up so long on boats, they were finally enjoying a small taste of freedom to create absolute chaos. We ate at long wooden tables that seemed to go on for miles, and were given typically American food, including milk and butter, which were impossible to find in Europe during the war. We felt as if we were in the Plaza Hotel. We had a place to sleep, food on the table, and the war was an ocean away. We were survivors, for now.

In the morning, we were awakened at six, given a towel and a bar of soap, and escorted to huge rooms of showers. It was the first time in months I had a hot shower. If you needed clothing, all you had to do was ask a social worker. During the day, one of the workers would wheel around a cart of cigarettes and candy. You could even get a Hungarian newspaper. All you needed was a little cash. I was in heaven. Despite these pleasures, we were reminded of our true circumstances at night, when the huge iron doors clanged shut and we were locked inside. In between, there was not much to do but be grateful for the sanctuary, and to try to figure out a way to get off the island and resume our lives.

There were thousands of refugees in Ellis Island, but only two public telephones. From the time we woke till the time we went to sleep, hundreds of people lined up to use the phones to try to contact somebody: relative, friend, or friend of a friend. The line seemed to stretch from here back to Europe. It was like waiting on line for Communion, each of us hoping for salvation.

For one hour in the afternoon, we were allowed to walk around the gardens. Everybody would line up and walk, while the guards stood watching us from their posts. You could practically touch Manhattan, but the distance between the two islands seemed to be measured in something greater than distance. Manhattan seemed worlds away.

Inside Ellis Island was a courtroom, where every day a judge would hear a certain number of cases, giving a certain number of people their freedom. When it came to be my turn I stood in front of the judge and the first thing he asked me was, "Why did you come to America?"

"Your honor," I said, "because there is a war in Europe, and I escaped."

I couldn't believe he could ask such a question! Did he think I was on vacation? This was hardly my idea of a good time.

I contacted a cousin from Budapest who had married an American navy captain and was living in San Francisco. At the time her husband was on the east coast, and he flew to New York to see what he could do on my behalf. Through his efforts, I was given a guarantee to sign that once freed from Ellis Island, I would leave the United States within two weeks. We left Ellis Island for Manhattan where we got a room at a hotel.

By now the war in Europe had intensified. We had very little money and even fewer prospects. I did however receive an invitation to dance in Shanghai from the impresario Strock, and Ariane and I decided to go to China. Strock was the Hurok of the Orient, with offices in Japan. Unfortunately, Ariane and I had to travel separately because her American ship refused me passage— my wonderful Hungarian passport again. I had to take a Dutch ship. Ariane and I were to meet in Manila before going on to Shanghai. There, we'd meet my sister Martha and her husband, the opera singer Désiré Ligeti, who had escaped from Hungary, too, and was now teaching in a conservatory in Manila.

Before I left New York, I realized that I had no professional photographs for my work, so I set about finding somebody who could take pictures of us. Among the people I asked was the then editor in chief of *Dance* magazine, Madame Dzermolinska, who told me, "I have a dancer who makes fantastic photography, and he needs the money. Let him do it."

"Where is he?" I asked.

"He's working now at Radio City Music Hall. Go to him and tell him that I sent you."

"What's his name?"

"Michael Kidd."

So Ariane and I went in search of this Michael Kidd. We tracked him down and he agreed to take our photos. We made an appointment to come to his studio, which I recall was in the very, very west forties or fifties on the top floor of a walk-up. I arrived with all of my costumes in a trunk and heaved my way up the stairs. It was a shabby place, darkly lit, with noises coming from the open windows of other apartments. His wife and child were in another room while Michael, extremely professional, shot the pictures in his living room. Ariane and I took turns posing in front of a black curtain. They were forwarded to me in the Philippines, with instructions on how to order more copies. I still have the note he enclosed. When, after the war, Michael became a big star, and we'd sometimes meet at a cafeteria on 57th Street, he was always down-to-earth and very kind. A leading dancer with American Ballet Theatre, he later was the Tony award-winning choreographer for *Finian's Rainbow*, *Guys and Dolls*, and *Can-Can*, among others.

We had been in the Philippines three weeks visiting my sister when war broke out in the Pacific. Ariane and I were then stranded in Manila for four years. Because it was an island, there was no place to run. The banks closed. We had no more money. For once, however, my Hungarian passport became an asset as the Japanese were of course allied with the Germans and Hungarians. After Pearl Harbor, later in December 1941, the Japanese began to bomb the Philippines, where there were very few shelters because so many of the houses had no basements. Every minute, a

My father.
Armin Szilard, 1946.

My mother.
Julia Szilard.

Paul Szilard. Five years old.

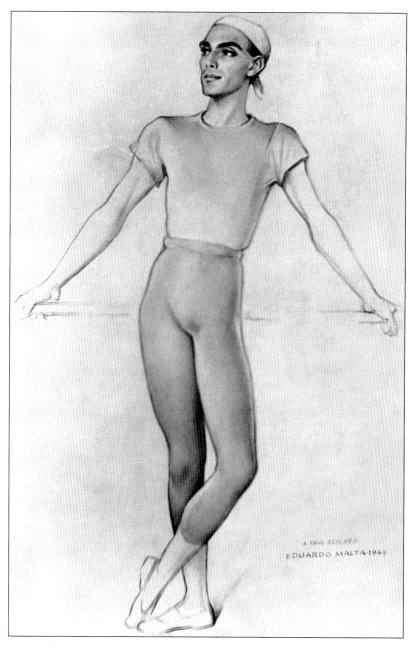

Author's portrait by famous Portuguese painter Eduardo Malta.

Portrait of my wife Ariane.

In *Les Patineurs,* which I choreographed.

Poster for Paul and Ariane Szilard's dance recital
in Geneva, Switzerland, in 1940.

As Albrecht, second act of *Giselle*.

Giselle, with Nora Kaye in Tokyo, Japan.

Photo: Minami

Crossing the Atlantic to Europe aboard the *New Amsterdam*,
with former stars of the Ballets Russes de Monte Carlo.

In *Haragos Férj* (The Angry Husband), a Hungarian
dance film shot in Budapest.

Performing a Farucca solo in Barcelona, Spain.

French stage and screen star Colette Marchand.

With Colette Marchand in Bartók's *The Miraculous Mandarin.*

New Year's Eve at the Imperial Hotel in Tokyo with Romola Nijinsky.

With Sonia Arova, performing at the San Carlos
Opera House in Lisbon, Portugal.

Opening Night Gala at San Carlos Opera House in Lisbon,
with composer Ernesto Halffter.

Melissa Hayden,
Prima Ballerina
of the New York
City Ballet.

Photo: Maurice Seymour

Violette Verdy,
Prima Ballerina of
New York City Ballet,
in Balanchine's
Allegro Brillante.

Jacques d'Amboise, star of New York City Ballet,
in Balanchine's *Tchaikovsky pas de deux*.

Patricia Neary, Principal Dancer of New York City Ballet, in rehearsal
with Balanchine, Jimmy Doolittle, and Lincoln Kirstein.

With Patricia Wilde, Prima Ballerina of the New York City Ballet, at Violette Verdy's wedding.

Reception for Violette Verdy at the French Consulate in New York City, with conductor Pierre Boulez, Violette, and George Balanchine.

bomb exploded. At the start of the war, the Japanese triumphantly occupied the Philippines and the Americans fled. We had no idea what was going on because there were no newspapers and, of course, no television. But one day, there was complete silence. The bombs had stopped.

When we heard that the American troops under General MacArthur were quitting the island, we all became terrified. In retreat, the Americans burned everything they could. Manila was in flames. It was like daylight all night long. The piers, filled with food and jeeps, were destroyed. We didn't know whether we'd live or die. Then one morning, we woke up and saw in the distance what looked like a cloud coming towards us. It was the Japanese army, arriving to occupy the Philippines. When they entered Manila, no one was allowed out of doors, but I decided to sneak out into our front garden and have a good look. I hid behind a tree, and what I saw was shocking. The soldiers had no shoes, only bandages wrapped around their feet. They were the poorest, shabbiest army imaginable. They looked as though they had already lost the war.

During the Japanese occupation, I was considered a friendly alien because of my Hungarian passport. Ariane, being Swiss, was considered neutral and was left alone. Many others were thrown into concentration camps. There was absolutely nothing left in the stores. You couldn't even find an aspirin. Money had very little value. Ariane, my sister, and I sold some jewelry to get food. We bought a sack of rice and hid it under the bed to keep it from looters or soldiers. Thieves used to climb in through windows, which, because this was the tropics, were always open. To prevent this, I rigged up an alarm, a wire with a bell on it, which would ring when somebody tried to come in through a window. The bell rang repeatedly during the occupation, like a doorbell to hell.

Slowly, things began to normalize under the Japanese. People went to work, drove their cars, walked in the streets. Many people collaborated with their captors to make money. The black market was thriving. But you couldn't call it a normal life, because the threat of death was always in the background.

We shared a house with Martha and Désiré, all of us living up-stairs, while I managed to convert some of the main floor into a studio. I was able to make a piece of wood into a decent barre. Ariane and I found a big, old mirror, and placed it in the front of the room. Désiré had a piano on loan from the Manila Academy of Music, where he had taught before the war broke out. Ariane played the piano for class, while I taught ballet. Soon my students included the children of the most famous people in Manila, in-cluding those of Senator Quirino (who later became president), Vice-President Osmeña, and the wealthiest family of all, the Aranetas. Some of the families were wealthy before the war, and they made sure they stayed that way through the occupation. Quirino at first worked for the Japanese. Later, he became the leader of the underground resistance against Japan. When the Japanese began to lose the war, they captured and imprisoned Quirino and killed his wife and three of his five children.

When the children of the president came to the studio, they would arrive in an enormous Cadillac marked with presidential flags. Other times, when they couldn't come to me, a car would be sent and I would be driven to the Malacañang Palace. There I taught in a room Quirino had converted into a ballet studio for his children. When I made a show for my pupils, I'd rehearse in the Palace, which I didn't think was anything special. It had a lot of phony antiques in the Louis XIV and XV style, and, like most homes in the tropics, was decorated with rattan and wicker. The teakwood furnishings, however, were fantastic. In the Philippines there was no middle ground: either you were rich or you were poor, and the war only highlighted the division between the two. It wasn't long before the chief of police was sending his children to my studio, and then the most powerful judge on the island. My school was like a junior version of the government.

Unfortunately, almost nobody had the money to pay for class. Even Quirino paid me with eggs and flour, which otherwise were impossible to find. I became a very popular teacher, the Ni-jinsky of Manila, I used to say, because there was nobody else. I became so popular that I was asked to stage a benefit for VSAC

50

(Volunteer Social Aid Committee), an organization very much like the Red Cross. Its president was Miss Sunico, my great friend and a prominent member of society. My pupils and I performed for the organization at the International Theater. The money earned by the benefit was given to VSAC to distribute, with the largest share secretly going to American soldiers and citizens who were in hiding.

One day a Japanese general and his entourage came to my studio to see what I was doing. They were always suspicious, and thinking something covert must be happening in the dance studio. The general told me he had heard about my show for VSAC and asked if I would do an entertainment for the sick and wounded Japanese soldiers. I felt I had no choice but to go along with their request and say yes, because the consequences would have been severe had I refused: they would have cut off my head. They named their terms and were willing to pay. I did the show for the Japanese, but the money they paid me I gave to VSAC to help the fugitive Americans.

On the day of the show thousands of people came to the theater. But instead of being dressed in their military garb, they were in their hospital clothes, as if they were pilgrims on their way to Lourdes to be cured. Busload after busload of wounded and maimed soldiers appeared. Nobody made a sound, but it's always like that in a Japanese theater. As a matter of fact, the general learned that the money raised was going to the American underground, but because the show was such a success and his soldiers were so entertained, he turned his back.

I hated to walk the streets because a Japanese soldier was stationed on every corner. In Japan, it is customary to acknowledge the presence of a soldier by stopping and bowing when you get to his station, as a courtesy to the military. This custom was brought to the Philippines, but I found it inconceivable to have to bow down to my captors. Many times I tried to avoid them by crossing the street, but if they saw me doing that I was stopped. "You, over there," they would yell, and I had no choice but to halt. When I did, I was slapped across the face and made to bow. These were the most humiliating and degrading times of my life.

When the Americans, led by General MacArthur, launched their return to Manila, the Japanese became desperate. The skies darkened with the American planes. I went out of the house one morning and took a shot of shrapnel in my arm, but it was not a lasting injury. During the death march, at the end of the Japanese occupation, I stood on the street and watched the dying stumble by me. Thousands of people were dragged through the streets only to be beaten, shot, or otherwise executed. The Japanese preferred the bayonet, and I watched in horror as a Japanese soldier beheaded a Filipino. Whatever life or spirit was left in these people was stomped out by the Japanese. It was the worst nightmare imaginable.

Every morning the sky grew black from the American bombers. Their assault began early, at precisely 7 A.M., as regular as clockwork, and there were very few places to hide. I would say to Ariane, who was showering before the 7 A.M. bombing, "Hurry up, the bombings are going to start any minute," and we still had to crawl under the house for shelter. Sometimes I'd find her exercising or playing the piano, and when I'd try to get her to move, she would resist, not wanting to let anything get to her.

"I am tired of going downstairs. I'd rather play the piano."

"Ariane," I'd say, "are you crazy? The bombs are going to start in a minute."

Sometimes, she wouldn't budge, and I'd be holed up beneath the house, listening to the sounds of bombs and Beethoven.

As the Americans relentlessly continued their bombing and things became progressively worse for the Japanese, they became more and more vicious to us. My sister and I got separated because she had a newborn baby and she wanted to be safe in hiding with a Filipino family. We didn't see her and Désiré again until after the war ended. One evening, the Japanese found Ariane and me and forced us out onto the street where they had rounded up other people. We had covered ourselves from head to toe, to make ourselves blend into the dark night, and we all carried a small bundle on our backs. Ariane got the attention of one of the soldiers and somehow made a hand gesture to indicate she had left her bundle in the garden and wanted to retrieve it. Leave it to the Swiss! I couldn't believe it, but she got the package and when she came back, we found ourselves at the end of the line.

Soon we could see that the Japanese were separating the men from the women. Men left, women right. At the time, I was sick, and wore a cloth around my head and shoulders that looked like a shawl. In the dark night, I could have been mistaken for a woman. Ariane was right behind me, and pushed me with her into the women's line. One woman on line turned around when she saw what Ariane had done, but Ariane said, "Shhh," and the woman turned back. The Japanese soldiers didn't notice that I was on the wrong line. The men spent the next few hours digging their own graves before being shot in the head.

The women were marched toward the hospital, where they were to be used by the Japanese as a shield against the American soldiers, spared only because they were temporarily worth more to the Japanese alive than dead. They expected to prevent the American soldiers from shooting because they would not want to kill innocent people.

The bombing had become unbearable. The night was deafening. The smell of smoke and blood was everywhere. We thought the hospital would be a safe haven, but, though the subterfuge that had brought me there went unnoticed, we were wrong. We believed that the Americans would not attack, because the Red Cross flag was flying at the top of the hospital. But the Japanese had placed guns inside the building.

We had no water and little food, and had trouble getting any of the bare necessities. There was no stove. You had to find some wood to build a fire, in order to boil water or cook some rice for dinner. We had with us a maid we called Aida, because she had very bushy hair and looked as if she came right out of the opera. She was fantastic in her loyalty and would not leave us. She'd go out and pick leaves off the trees and boil them in water to make a kind of soup.

I became very sick from nerves and felt that I was on the way to a breakdown. All around us people were screaming but we couldn't move. The Japanese soldiers would grab women at random, drag them into the corner of the room, and rape them. They'd take children away from their mothers, then rape the mother after throwing the child up in the air and having it land on a bayonet. We were lying on the floor of the hospital and I was sickened by the smell of the dead and the dying around me. Suddenly, I felt warm on one side of my body, and looked down to see that blood was spilling from one side of the room, soaking my hospital gown and continuing to ooze around me. Still I could not move.

Later, the nights went eerily silent. There was no more bombing, no more screaming. We were amazed. We didn't know what had happened. Now I felt that if I was going to hang on to my sanity, whatever remained, I needed to keep up some kind of routine. So at some point, I started shaving, Ariane helping me by holding up a piece of broken mirror. My doctor, an Austrian émigré who was with us in the hospital, couldn't believe that I was shaving at such a moment. "Who shaves at a time like this?" he asked Ariane. He thought it was the first sign of a nervous collapse.

Shortly after, the tallest man we had seen in a long time walked in. We were like animals who burrow down in the dirt, and are blinded by first daylight. He told us to come out. He was an American soldier. We couldn't believe it. Evidently, the war was coming to an end. I was glad I had shaved.

Everyone around me started screaming, "The Americans are back! The Americans are back!" People threw themselves at the soldier's feet. There was shouting and crying.

The Americans took us by truck to an abandoned church, where we slept on mattresses or on the floor. We were given tins of sardines or tuna fish. We ate those for weeks. The sight of a sardine today is enough to make me lose my appetite.

When we finally left the church one afternoon, Manila was unrecognizable. It had been flattened by the war but had become a mountain of dead bodies, with corpses everywhere. One of the most chilling sensations of that time was the sound of trucks and tanks crushing the bones of the dead. When I think back to those days, I can still hear it. Everything we had come to know in our years there had vanished. It was as if we had left the church and entered another world. Ariane and I, with what few possessions we wore or held in our hands, walked on a bombed-out road, but we had no idea in what direction we were heading. We had no shoes, only rags we had managed to wrap around our feet like bandages. We looked at each other as if we were the first man and woman in the world, or possibly the last. Where could we go?

After walking for a mile or so, we passed a house that had been bombed but was still standing. One side of the building was gone, and we could look up into the exposed rooms, the way you can look into a child's doll's house.

"This is where we shall stay for the time being," I told Ariane, and we walked into the shell of the building, up a flight of stairs to the room we had seen from the street. It was completely open to the hot, smoky Manila night. In the morning, people would walk by on the street, wave to us, and say hello.

Within a few days I began to search for my old pupils, not to resume teaching, but to find out what had happened to them, because many had become friends. But what I learned was horrible. Many were killed, including a Spanish girl who was one of six children in a family. The Japanese had come into their home, tied them up, poured gasoline over them, then lit the fire and walked away.

The Japanese even burned to the ground a club that was owned and frequented by Germans, their supposed friends. By the end of the war, they didn't care whom they were killing.

When the war had first started, Ariane and I had put our music and costumes in an iron trunk that we buried as deep as we could in the backyard of our house. We covered that with a marble top. With the war ended, we got some local boys to help us and we started digging. Of course, our house itself was destroyed, with nothing left but a few remnants of wall. But once we found that, we began to excavate. Finally, after digging and digging, we found the costumes and music and then, all of a sudden, everything went up in flames. We had come this far, had uncovered what we had buried, and right in front of us, these flames claimed everything the war hadn't. Except ashes. Somehow, deadly heat had been trapped inside that burial place. Ariane started to cry; I put my arm around her and said, "Don't cry. We are alive."

"From now on," I told Ariane, "I don't want to have any belongings. I want to live with what I have, but I don't want material things anymore." I had heard of people who did not leave Germany because they could not part with their piano. Instead of running away, they were shipped off to concentration camps.

When General MacArthur returned triumphant to the Philippines, I was asked to put together a gala at the Manila hotel to celebrate American reoccupation. I organized the entire evening and was even asked to dance. Dance? Aside from my teaching, I hadn't moved for three years. By this time we had found another house to stay in: a rich Swiss friend, Mrs. Parson, whose house had been far enough from town not to have been damaged by bombing, had given us the use of her house.

Provost Marshall O'Brian, a doctor from New England, was in charge of the reoccupation and soon became a very close friend of ours. "What do you need for the performance?" he asked.

"Ballet shoes," I said. "I have nothing."

It wasn't long before I got an enormous package that contained one hundred pairs of ballet shoes and an enormous number of toe shoes and tights.

"O.B.," I said (that's what we called O'Brian), "I didn't think you were going to order this much."

"This is the army. You can't expect me to order one pair of shoes. It's just not done. Anything else?"

"Well, I need a stage. And lights."

"What kind of lights do you need?" he asked, and when I tried to explain, he said, "All right, all right."

I should have been a bit more specific. When I stood on the platform specially built for this occasion and asked for the lights, I'll never forget the shock I felt when a pair of huge searchlights, the kind used to scan the sky for airplanes, were turned on.

Needless to say, anyone on the stage was swallowed up by so much light that they couldn't see.

Generals from all the different branches of the military came to watch the show, for which I choreographed a ballet called *The Four Seasons*. O.B. considered the performance such a hit that he had another idea for me. He wanted me to open a bar for officers in Manila and promised he would get us all the supplies we needed. It was very important for the army to have an officer's club, because the Philippines remained so dangerous that American soldiers were being poisoned in local bars by Japanese soldiers who hadn't surrendered. There were still such Japanese snipers and Filipino collaborators hiding everywhere. I once saw a U.S. serviceman writhing on the street, screaming from pain after he had had a drink that left him blind and hysterical. Strict orders were handed down that no soldier could drink in a bar (some G.I.'s managed to get liquor at streetside shacks). But an officer's club is controlled and I would buy the liquor from the PX.

With O.B.'s help, I opened "The Blue Elephant" and it became the sensation of Manila. I had found two decorative blue elephants in the market, named the club for them, and placed them in the garden. I had no experience at all in running a bar or a club, which made its success all the more wonderful. Neither Ariane nor I drank. When we first opened our doors, a soldier would order a fancy drink like a gin fizz, and Ariane and I would look at each other, because we didn't know what he was talking about. A soldier would ask for a club sandwich, and we would go around looking for clubs. It became a great joke! And soon we were telling the soldiers to come behind the bar and fix drinks and food themselves. Gradually, we learned how to make the drinks and sandwiches, and eventually the club proved a great source of personal satisfaction. Plus, we made a lot of money. But we couldn't have done it without O.B.

Every day at the Blue Elephant brought a different adventure. One evening, having run out of Coca-Cola, we were in desperate need of the cola syrup we could only get the from the army. Our friend Noa, who was living with us, had a boyfriend named

Tommy, a captain in the army, but better still, he worked at the PX. During a blackout, he went to the PX at about one in the morning, took an entire barrel of Coca-Cola syrup, put it on his jeep, and brought it to the Blue Elephant. When he arrived, we almost died, because there was absolutely no place to conceal the evidence. We tried and tried to hide the barrel, but it was useless. We'd roll it one way and it would immediately roll back. We'd push and get nowhere while we almost split our sides with laughter. Desperate, we decided we had no hiding place for the Coca-Cola except upstairs in Noa's bedroom. But how were we to get it up there? Somehow, laughing and crying, we finally succeeded. But now with the Coca-Cola upstairs, we faced the problem of getting the cola syrup down to the bar. We had forgotten about that.

Noa had an idea, and, unfortunately, we had no choice but to watch her as she took her douche bag, squeezed out the air, and dipped it in the barrel, filling it with the Coca-Cola syrup. Again and again the bag was rushed downstairs and emptied at the bar.

In addition to food and drink, the Blue Elephant featured a pianist and dancing, which brought us a different kind of clientele, among them a lot of local transvestites. The soldiers would ask us, "Is that a man or a woman?" and often we couldn't answer for sure. When American soldiers returned to Manila by ship, they docked at a pier where there was a hospital that offered them inoculations against syphilis and gonorrhea. On one side of the pier were the gay boys, on another the whores, and on the third the transvestites, all waiting for their "clients" to come out of the hospital.

On Christmas Day we wanted to have a party and O.B. helped by supplying the food: about half a dozen fresh turkeys and a case each of real eggs, butter, and cheese. We hadn't seen or eaten any of these in years.

"How did you get it?" I asked him.

He smiled and answered, "A Red Cross ship came in. I went to inspect the kitchen and made them open the refrigerator. When I found something that we could use for our party, I yelled 'Out! That's rotten and stinks!'"

We didn't know what to do with it all. There were at least two hundred eggs. We gave most of them away to our friends. "Why so many eggs?" I asked O.B.

"I couldn't very well ask for two," he said.

In 1945, it was impossible for us to get back to the United States. There was no transportation available since, first, all the soldiers who had served in the Philippines needed to get home, and second, Americans who had been interned in Japanese concentration camps needed to be repatriated. Obviously, their needs took precedence over ours, leaving us no chance to find a way out.

After a year of our living in limbo, O.B. agreed it was time for us to return to the United States. We had the money for the trip, thanks to the Blue Elephant, but we didn't have the visas. When we explained our situation to O.B., we could practically see the wheels turning in his head. He had an idea. The next day we were introduced to an American lawyer, a good friend of O.B.'s who had come to the Philippines to reestablish American banks. He sent a telegram to the State Department in Washington, D.C., vouching for us. A few months later we had the visas in our hands. That was a good first step. Unfortunately, we still couldn't get passage on a ship. We explained this to O.B., who thought about it for a moment and came up with a plan: he was going to sneak us on an army ship, all of which were strictly for the repatriation of American soldiers. O.B. had managed to get my sister Martha and her baby a seat on a DC–3, but there was no room for Ariane and me. Now, though we were going to be stowaways, O.B. felt that since we had valid visas, once we got to the United States we'd be allowed to stay.

Ariane and I were scared and reluctant to do this, but he insisted we go. It was our only way off the island. If we didn't follow his plan, there was a chance that we'd be stuck in the Philippines for years.

"Go," he said, and we went.

He made a deal with the captain of a Red Cross ship and, late one night, we arrived on the docks with our baggage. Most of our

things were in a wooden Chinese trunk. In the darkness, he secretly got us on board while no one was around, and locked Ariane in the captain's cabin, in his toilet. I was locked up in some
other bathroom. We were not to show our faces until we were out
at sea. What could they do then with two stowaways in the middle of the ocean?

All went according to plan until the captain got cold feet and
called the police, who removed us from the ship the next morning. The ship was crammed with sick and disabled soldiers who
filled every inch of available space. We had to walk out in front of
everybody, who watched us walk the bridge. I was so ashamed
there were tears in my eyes. When we finally saw O.B. again, I
said, "Don't you ever put us on another ship." Of course, that remained our only way of leaving Manila.

Sometime later O.B. found another soldiers' repatriation ship
on which we would not be stowaways, though Ariane and I were
the only two civilians and she the only woman on board. One of
the officers gave Ariane his cabin, from which she was not allowed
to leave. I stayed in a cabin with three soldiers, two to a bunkbed.
Many evenings Ariane and I dragged our mattresses from our cab-
ins and slept on deck.

It took about thirty-five days to reach the United States. The
reason the ship went so slowly was the fear of mines, and, although the war was over, the fear of soldiers who hadn't surrendered. Every night there would be a blackout, and we were not
even allowed to smoke on the deck and perhaps reveal our presence to nighttime snipers in the air or at sea. Only if we moved
very slowly was it possible for special scouts at the front of the
ship to check the waters for mines and if spotted shoot and disable
them. Every day aboard ship, there was the screaming of "mines,
mines," and then the sound of explosions as the soldiers destroyed
the mines. The ship moved as slowly as if we were walking.

We landed in Seattle, Washington, and as soon as we could
Ariane and I went down to San Francisco to join my sister
Martha and her family, who had left the Philippines earlier. Her
husband, Désiré Ligeti, had escaped on a merchant marine ship

and was engaged by the San Francisco Opera when he reached the United States.

We stayed at the St. Francis Hotel and, without any real clothes, looked like hobos, Ariane wearing a soldier's coat whose sleeves were about a foot longer than her arms. When we went down to the shop in the hotel lobby we felt like children in a candy store. It had been so long since we had seen new clothing, let alone worn any. Ariane tried on dresses while I picked up slacks and shirts. Both of us needed shoes and sweaters and most everything else. The shopkeeper was ecstatic, saying he hadn't seen a sale like this since before the war. As I've mentioned, we had made a lot of money at the Blue Elephant, and I now spent it freely on clothes. Ariane threw out her old coat, and we began to look like our old selves again, the selves we hadn't seen in years. We walked the new city in our new clothes, wondering what the next act of our lives would bring.

PART II

THE DANCE RESUMES

NOT TOO LONG AFTER WE ARRIVED IN SAN FRANCISCO, we decided to go back to New York City, where I would try to pick up my dance career. Because I hadn't danced in a long time and was completely out of shape, I knew I first had to find a class, which I did at the Ballet Arts in Carnegie Hall. It took time to get back into shape—after all, I wasn't young any more—but after studying at Ballet Arts, I began to teach, make contacts, and receive offers to dance with other companies.

I got an offer to teach in Texas—I can't remember the name of the town—and was asked to come down for an interview. I had very little money, so I traveled mostly by bus. In any event, I arrived at the bus station in that town and when I got to the bathroom I saw one sign for blacks and another for whites. Then when I got on a local bus, I noticed the blacks had to sit in the back. When I said hello to these black people, they didn't say hello back, as if they were hardly accustomed to being recognized as people. I thought, how can human beings be treated like this?

In Hungary, we had no black people. And it was beyond my understanding that whites should hate black people. I was so disgusted by this that when I came back to New York, I told my wife that I'd rather wash dishes at Horn and Hardart than accept going to a place where there was such discrimination. I couldn't understand it, because for me everybody was and is the same.

From the time I first heard about the lynchings and all the other offenses against blacks, I just couldn't stand that. I love America and I became an American—probably I'm more American than the Americans—but even today I cannot accept such discrimination. I give money to organizations like the Southern

Poverty Law Center and while I don't say there's been no improvement, I still cannot understand, for instance, why newspapers have to refer to a new judge "who is black." They don't say a new judge "who is white," they just say, "a new judge."

Teaching Ballet

Soon after the war, I taught not only at Ballet Arts in Carnegie Hall but also at schools in various cities around the U.S. In those days dance teaching was at an all-time low, an absolute circus outside Manhattan. Because people were uneducated in dance, with very few credentials, you could get a certificate through the mail to teach it. In the smaller towns, this kind of dance class was thriving, while in New York, the dance teachers were starving. I don't know how some schools were allowed to open. Today, of course, all that has changed, and there are, indeed, many fine dance schools all over the country.

Many of the boys I taught came to me on the G.I. bill, but few seemed particularly interested in dancing. When I asked them why they came to class, they said that they were there to meet girls or boys, depending on what they wanted.

While at Ballet Arts, I was invited to teach at a school in a small American city that shall remain nameless. I packed my overnight bag and left. When I arrived, there was an enormous, long studio, and the woman who invited me, and who was rather fat, sat at one end. She carried a long stick. Her use of the French terminology was terrible, and I could hardly understand what she was saying. The room was packed with students. When it was time for me to teach, she placed all of her pupils in three lines: beginners, intermediate, and advanced. The first line of girls wore patent leather shoes and frilly white dresses. "When are they changing?" I asked. And the woman on the bench told me, "Oh, heavens no. They go right to church after this." I was beginning to boil over. The only thing that could get me through the class was thinking about the money I was making. I turned to ask for the pianist and was told,

"Oh, heavens, no, Mr. Zee-lord, we don't have a piano, we have a jukebox." I couldn't believe it. It wasn't even a tape recorder.

All the parents, grandparents, and siblings of the children taking class had come into the studio to watch the teacher from Carnegie Hall. "Money," I said to myself, "Just think of the money." I began the class, and then all of a sudden I heard a loud whoosh and thud coming from a corner of the room. It was the Coca-Cola machine dispensing soft drinks in the middle of my class. That was it. I couldn't take it anymore. I went to the lady and said, "Madam, I am so sorry. You can keep your money, but I am leaving." I grabbed my coat and walked out.

In the same city, but in a different school, Leon Danielian of the Ballets Russes de Monte Carlo was teaching. We were very good friends and planned to have dinner after we had both taught our classes. I told him I'd come to his studio. When I got there, he was still teaching in a huge gymnasium. There must have been at least one hundred pupils in the class. Students were lined up at the barre and he was telling them to bend their knees and sink down, then rise up. "Go down, and come up." He was talking to them as if they were idiots. I said to him, "Why don't you use the word plié?"

"Are you out of your mind?" Danielian said. "They wouldn't know what the hell I'm talking about. I don't give a damn. I get two dollars a pupil."

We went to dinner together and talked about our teaching experiences. We didn't know whether we should laugh or cry. Of course, today the situation is completely different.

The director of Ballet Arts was Miss Lee. She was an unbelievable character, sometimes kind and sometimes a monster. She and I got on quite well, and after she hired me, she hired Kyra Nijinsky on my recommendation. When we were teaching, we didn't get a regular salary. Every time a pupil took class, half the payment went to Ballet Arts, half to the teacher. But Miss Lee always cheated us, cutting down our money as much as she could. But she did have fantastic teachers like Nina Stroganova and Vladimir Dokoudovsky. And everybody came to those classes, from Cyd Charisse to Agnes de Mille to Jacques d'Amboise.

One day Miss Lee told me that I was a very good teacher and I should open up my own school in the suburbs to make some money. She suggested Bay Shore, on Long Island. "Why Bay Shore?" I asked. "Well, I can't stand to go outside of New York City. You try it."

So I decided to give Bay Shore a try. I opened up a very proper ballet studio one flight below a ballroom dancing school. The local people turned out to be the most provincial people when it came to dance. Mothers arrived with their little Pavlovas and were very demanding. "I would like to have my six-year-old daughter take private class," one woman said to me. "I don't recommend it at that age. She might find it quite boring to be on her own. What has she done?" I asked.

"Well, last year she did *Swan Lake* at the school recital, and this year I would very much like for her to dance *Carmen*."

"I don't think we'll have a recital because we've just opened. Probably in about two years," I said.

In those days I charged a lot of money because I was trying to discourage most of these children from attending. I asked ten dollars for private lessons.

"Miss Marcy on the other side of town only charges three dollars," the mother protested.

"Well, Madam, then you must go to her," I said.

"How about half an hour?" she said.

"OK," I said, finally giving in.

"But I don't want her to have any more barres because she had that last year. I want her to have tap, ballet, and baton twirling," she said.

"All in a half hour?" I asked.

"Of course," she said.

"In that case Madam, you are in the wrong place, and must return to Miss Marcy."

It didn't take me long to realize that this wasn't for me. I felt distraught. I thought I was too good for this. I was disgusted with the dilettantes. I went to the woman who rented the studio to me, gave her the key, and said "Goodbye."

I had only one pupil, about fifteen years old, who had any talent. She wanted to be a figure skater. Her mother begged me not to quit, and one day, she picked me up in a Rolls-Royce, drove me to her estate, and told me that I had to stay in Bay Shore because she wanted a professional teacher for her daughter. She was willing to pay all my expenses for half a year if only I'd agree to continue.

"Madam," I said, "with all due respect, there is not enough money on the entire island to keep me here for that long. I'd love to teach class to your daughter, because she's talented, but she has to come to New York."

I have no patience for people who are mediocre and have no talent. I don't mind spending time with somebody with talent. But I cannot stand amateurism or things halfway-done. Even in cooking! I certainly cannot stand amateurs in art. Once I was in a position where I could choose, I would only accept professionals. And I can be rude about it: I don't mind firing somebody. There are so many professionals who are good but don't have jobs. So often the ones who get the job are the amateurs, and the pros are the ones who don't! In my opinion, sometimes the people who hire are amateurs themselves.

I'm especially against bad teachers. They take a couple of classes and think they can teach. It's like a building; it collapses if the base is wrong. In ballet, especially, you cannot put a child on her toes until she's physically ready; you can't do it just because the mother likes to see the child hopping up on a toe. Many times ballet teachers do terrible damage to the child because they want to please the parent or because they need to make money. Years ago, when Alvin Ailey invited me to see classes, the teachers were generally not very good. I'd criticize him for this and he would get angry, saying, "OK, if you don't like it, why don't you teach yourself?" "No, I wouldn't teach here, it's your school," I used to tell him. Of course, today the Ailey company has excellent teachers.

Agnes de Mille

One time shortly after the war when I needed a job as a dancer, I auditioned for a Broadway show choreographed by Agnes de Mille. I can't remember what show it was. After I danced Agnes looked at me and said, "You are a good dancer but I cannot use you because you have too much personality. I need somebody for the *corps de ballet*."

Later on we became something like friends, but she got annoyed because I never approached her to be her impresario. When she had her own company in the 1950s, she wanted me to book her in Europe and so on. Another time many years later, when she was old and already paralyzed, she invited me to her home and said to me, "I can't understand you. You never do anything for me. Why do you do everything for Alvin and nothing for me?"

I said, "Well, let's see what I can do."

But I really didn't want to, and I never did. I like to do things I believe in, because then I know how to sell it. I hated all those too-Americanized ballets she did. They were not for me. I liked her, but she could be a very unpleasant lady.

Katherine Dunham

During my teaching career, when I was giving class at Ballet Arts in Carnegie Hall, I received a telephone call from the manager of the Katherine Dunham company. She wanted to know if I'd be available to teach ballet to the Dunham dancers. It wasn't unusual for a modern or theatrical company to want to have ballet instruction for its dancers. In this case, ballet was a secondary subject in the school, because the main subject was the Katherine Dunham technique. I was interested in the position not only because I felt that Dunham was one of the great dancers of the time, but also, frankly, because I needed a job.

Dunham was beautiful and elegant and had her own style of

dance. Dancer, choreographer, anthropologist, and activist, Dunham combined Caribbean dance, ballet, and African rituals with African-American rhythms to create her technique. Not only was she known for her show *Tropics and Le Jazz Hot*, but she had also appeared in the Broadway musical *Cabin in the Sky*, choreographed by Balanchine. She later had the honor of being the first African-American to choreograph for the Metropolitan Opera when, in 1963, she provided the dances for their production of *Aida*.

When I started teaching at her school, I only had a few pupils, but when word got around that I wasn't so bad my classes began to fill up. In fact, so many students began showing up that I stayed at the Dunham school for almost three years. I left to devote more time to my own dancing and choreography. During that period, I taught many of the Dunham dancers who would later make names for themselves on Broadway, including Harry Belafonte and Eartha Kitt.

San Carlos Opera, Portugal

Sometime not long after the war I returned to Portugal to perform as a guest artist at the Coliseum. I went to Paris in search of a partner, and spoke to my old friend from prewar Paris, the famous artist Serge Lifar, who was the *maître de ballet* of the Paris Opera (and for whom Balanchine had choreographed *Apollo*). "Serge, I need a good young dancer to be my partner. Do you know anyone?" I asked.

"Come tomorrow night," he said, "I'm dancing with a girl at a gala. Her name is Sonia Arova. She's not a member of the Paris Opera. Nobody knows who she is . . . yet. She's twenty-three years old and a sensation. You will love her."

Sonia was born in Bulgaria, and began her dance training at the school of the Sofia Opera Ballet. She left Bulgaria at the age of eleven, with her mother, to further her studies in Paris. Though she fled to England during the war, she had returned to Paris as soon as she could.

Lifar was right. When I went to see Sonia, I was mesmerized. She had a strong personality, and a flawless technique. She was an excellent artist and extremely musical. This was just the kind of partner I needed. I immediately signed her to come to Lisbon to dance two ballets with me: *Les Sylphides* and a new ballet I had choreographed, *Mephisto Waltz*, to music by Liszt. We were getting along beautifully, and then she came to me one afternoon and said that she would like to dance a Spanish solo number on the program. I told her, "Sonia, it is impossible. We are already dancing two numbers in one night. We have to give the local dancers a chance. We'll do something another time." But Sonia kept insisting on a Spanish solo number, which I could not accept.

When we got to the general rehearsal with *Sylphides*, I was standing at the rear of the stage with Sonia and another ballerina, all of us in the customary classical balletic pose. When the curtain opened, suddenly I heard Spanish music. I couldn't believe my ears. Sonia left us and went to the middle of the stage to do her solo. I felt like an idiot. I stopped the rehearsal and asked both Sonia and the conductor, "What's going on?"

"It's a rehearsal for my Spanish number," Sonia said, "I spoke to the director and he said I could do it."

"And you said nothing and let me stand in the back like an idiot? How could you do that?" I was furious. "I don't want to dance with you anymore," I said, "You're out. Finished." I was so mad that I threw her out of rehearsal and called the understudy to step in. The management got hysterical; they had already sold tickets with Sonia as a guest artist, and they insisted that she dance. I had no choice but to accept the situation and dance with her. However, we didn't say one word to each other during the entire engagement. I wanted nothing to do with her. It took time before we would resume our friendship.

Later on, Sonia came to America, and partnered Rudolf Nureyev in the *Don Quixote pas de deux* at the Brooklyn Academy of Music in 1962, for his debut in the U.S. Both Sonia and Rudi were sensational.

When Sonia became a member of American Ballet Theatre, I

booked her and her husband, Thor Sutowski, as guest artists for a production of *Sleeping Beauty* with the Komaki Ballet of Japan. I went to Tokyo to attend those performances. During intermission one evening, I got a message that I should immediately come backstage because the dancer who was playing the evil Carabosse had had an attack of some kind and couldn't go on. Sonia said to me, "You have to come and jump in." I never in my life had danced *Sleeping Beauty*. She said "There's no alternative, there's nobody. Just do whatever you can onstage." Since there was no understudy for the role, I had no choice but to get into the costume. As I was being made up, I told Sonia, "Onstage, don't do anything but glissade arabesque with me." It's the simplest step in ballet. "Don't do anything else because I don't know what in the hell I'm going to do." When I finished my debut with Sonia, I was pushed out in the cart, while the mice started running around me. They pushed me here and they pushed me there. When I wasn't holding on for dear life, I managed some wonderful *ports de bras*. Eventually, I was rolled off the stage, and the act was saved.

Erik Bruhn

Through Sonia Arova, I met Erik Bruhn, who later became my client for three years. Originally with the Royal Danish Ballet, he was a phenomenal dancer, a strong technician as well as a strong dramatic presence. He was the top classical dancer of his time, perhaps of all time. He was the prince of classical ballet.

The first time we met was at the Wacker Studio in Paris. He was a very closed person, reluctant to discuss his private life. At one point, there was a big love affair between Sonia Arova and Erik. She wanted to marry him, but, of course, nothing happened. The whole thing cooled off.

Many years later, when I was an impresario, I suggested to Erik that he come under my representation. He thought that was a good idea, and I signed him up immediately. Even though I adored him, he was one of the most difficult artists to negotiate for. He had a mental block that made it hard for him to decide whether to accept an engagement or not. Once when I negotiated a proposition from the Marquis de Cuevas's company, which wanted Erik to guest with them, it took him a long time to agree. But a few mornings after he signed the contract, he called me sounding desperate. "Paul, I changed my mind. Can you get me out of the contract?" He thought he could just walk away. I canceled the contract. This happened several times and after three years of such headaches, I thought it was best just to be friends with Erik. "It's very difficult for me, Erik. Why don't we separate from business and just remain friends." He agreed, but said he would regret it, and we stayed friends.

When Erik became a member of New York City Ballet, he told me several times that he did not feel at home in the company and did not like the repertoire he had to dance. I remember specifically when he did not feel comfortable dancing Balanchine's *Theme and Variations* and was thinking of leaving the company. Shortly after, he quit. He preferred to dance with American Ballet Theatre because he felt much more comfortable with their repertory.

When Erik danced with Carla Fracci, they became one of the great partnerships in the history of classical ballet. Of course they danced beautifully during the performances, but they also became famous for the elaborate way they took their bows when the ballet ended. It really was a second show. People went insane with applause because Erik and Carla turned the bowing into pure theater. Their curtain calls were so fantastic that people came in just to see the end of the show.

Becoming an Impresario

In the early 1950s, at home in America, I was approached by the director of Japan's most famous ballet company, the Komaki, to come to Japan and be a guest artist with his company. Mr. Komaki, the director for whom the company was named, wanted me to stage *Swan Lake* and *Giselle*, as well as dance in both. Having danced those ballets in Europe, I felt I'd be able to stage the productions without any problem. At that time, the Japanese had very specific tastes. They wanted to see *Swan Lake* and *Giselle*. Nothing else. That was, and in many ways still is, their definition of dance. I was grateful for Mr. Komaki's offer, but told him I needed a few days before I could give him an answer.

I was at first hesitant to agree, because it was so soon after the war and I still could not forget everything that had happened to me at the hands of the Japanese soldiers. Granted, I got off easy compared to the ruined lives of countless others. All the same, this remained the only thing holding me back from giving Mr. Komaki an immediate yes. But, after some time, I realized that I had to separate art from politics in order to get on with my own life. Art had nothing to do with war. Art didn't make men into soldiers or put weapons in their hands. Art had nothing to do with killing, or torture, or the destruction of people's lives. I had always admired traditional Japanese theater such as Kabuki, and I respected the history of their theatrical traditions. On this basis, I decided to accept Mr. Komaki's invitation.

I was asked to bring a partner with me, and I approached Nora Kaye, who agreed to dance with me in Japan. So for this period of my life, I was a performer, a choreographer, and an impresario all rolled into one.

In those days, an impresario was a rare commodity in the Orient. I was highly appreciated as the only impresario who came over from America. Later on, many other agents came to Japan from America and Europe. Over time the life of an impresario in the Orient, however, has completely changed. Today, the Japanese don't need us anymore. They've become impresarios themselves.

When I returned from Japan, I decided to stop dancing and give all my time to becoming an impresario. In 1954 I opened a one-room office in the Fisk Building, on West 57th Street, and started my life as an impresario.

The Impresario Business

I am both impresario and producer because I both book the attractions and invest money in the production. The difference between a booking agent and an impresario is that the impresario produces the show and takes financial responsibility. Many impresarios have financial backers and they just act for them. I have sometimes had backers, especially when I was starting out. When I took Nora Kaye on a tour it was always paid for by a backer or a local company. When I worked with the Dancers of Bali, Columbia Management backed me up. But now I usually put in my own money, like a producer.

There are two ways attractions are booked. One way is for the booking agent to make a contract with the attraction, whereby he pays them the fee they ask for, and then sells them for a higher amount; that markup is his income. The other way is when the booking agent makes a contract with an attraction, which then pays him an agent's fee for every appearance he arranges. The standard agent fee in America—if you are honest—is 15%. Most of the people are not so honest and they ask 20% or more. And certain artists, when they are in serious need of an impresario or agent, will sign a contract with an agency for a 50-50 or 40-60 split of the fee earned. That's like stealing, because nothing remains for the artist after he pays his taxes and expenses. In Europe the standard agent's fee is 10%. I've reached the point in my life where I don't run after money. I always keep in mind that I was an artist once myself, and because I don't want to take advantage of people, I charge them barely what they must pay.

Today many impresarios ask the agent's fee and then, in addition to this, require the attraction to cover their expenses, like travel, telephone, taxes, and so on. I am very stupid because I don't do this. When I book a company, I ask only my 15%, and I don't care if I pay a little out of my own pocket. Sometimes, though, I burn my hands. Travel is very expensive and I go to many places all over the world. I always fly the Concorde to Europe because I don't like to sit eight hours in a plane, and after landing in Paris or London I can fly anywhere else in Europe in three-and-a-half hours or less. I could have charged for the Concorde but I never did. I always asked those clients who agreed to cover transportation to pay me for business class and I would make up the difference.

Unfortunately now, in the 21st century, fewer and fewer impresarios actually book attractions and take them on the road, because it is so expensive. You cannot be an impresario if you have no money. Just to run an office is very expensive. Some people may think that when an agent gets paid, all the money stays in his pocket. But the agent has to pay income taxes, office expenses, travel, hotel, and entertainment expenses, which are only partially tax-deductible. We negotiate and do other business in restaurants. And not at McDonald's! To go to a proper place costs a fortune today.

Some people ask me why I book clients only in foreign countries and not in America. I used to book in the United States, of course. When I produced and booked the Bunraku, the Japanese puppet theater, they were sold out, standing room only, in New York and all across the country. The tour finished in California, and I then called my company manager to find out what the final net outcome was. It turned out that after such an important sold-out eight-week tour and after deducting all the expenses, what remained was about a dollar and a half! I said to myself, if I cannot make money on such a hit nationwide, I don't want to be involved in any more tours in the United States.

But there is still another reason why I stopped booking in the U.S. I am completely against how some agencies are taking advantage of foreign companies that have no union regulations at home: they are taking the poor dancers on ten- or twelve-week bus tours of one-night stands. In principle, I am against one-night stands, even though they are necessary sometimes for financial reasons. Only a very large company can afford not to be booked for some one-night stands. You can't put an unknown company for three or four performances in places where there's no public for it. But too many one-night stands ruin the poor dancers. After sitting for I don't know how many hours on the buses, they sometimes, practically speaking, have to perform immediately. They don't have time to properly make up and their legs are swollen. When they get back home, they are practically ruined. Demolished.

Usually I am very popular among the dancers in a dance company. I act like a friend with them. I am like their father. Sometimes they come to me and tell me their most private stories, their love affairs. I don't know how many times I've given money to dancers who could not pay the rent or their prescription medicine bills. I've bought so many vitamins I could open a shop!

There are always unexpected problems with dancers on tour and they always came to me to solve them. I'm the fix-it man. One time in Paris, the last performance of the Ailey company's engagement at the Palais des Sports fell on a Sunday. We had to leave the country the following day. Suddenly I got a telephone call from the company manager telling me that one of our male dancers had lost his passport. How could I save the situation? In desperation, I managed to get the American ambassador on the telephone at his home. He somehow arranged for the American consulate to issue a new passport that same Sunday. We were elated that the problem was solved.

But then later on that evening I got a frantic phone call from the same dancer to tell me that he had lost the passport *again*! He had a bunch of postcards to mail and in dropping them into a postal box he accidentally threw the passport in the box with them. Somehow, through the intervention of some important people I knew in Parisian theater management, I was able to reach the General Postmaster at his home at night. He told me to get the number of the mailbox the dancer had thrown the passport in and to rush the number to the main post office. We followed those instructions, someone from the post office drove to the box, opened it up, and there—amidst what seemed like thousands of pieces of mail—was the passport!

Nora Kaye

In 1953, when I approached Nora Kaye to dance with me in Japan at the invitation of Mr. Komaki, she was already a star with both American Ballet Theatre and New York City Ballet, which she had joined in the spring of 1951 and left three years later. With ABT, she made her reputation in ballets such as *Lilac Garden, Pillar of Fire,* and *Fall River Legend,* and was an unqualified hit in Jerry Robbins's *The Cage.* We had been acquaintances for quite a while, but were not yet friends. She was very intrigued by my background and schooling as a dancer. She had watched me dance in class and knew what I could do. We'd meet often for coffee and talk about dance. I think she enjoyed those meetings, because, unfortunately, it's rare to find a dancer who can talk about anything but himself.

Although we had never danced together, Nora was clearly interested in being my partner at the Komaki. I told her that I wanted to dance *Giselle* and *Swan Lake*, that I had been coached in Europe and knew *Giselle* as it was done at the Paris Opera. I talked to her about the staging as I saw it. Nora's eyes lit up, and she accepted my invitation to Japan.

Through Nora I got to know Antony Tudor and his partner Hugh Laing. Since I was always bitchy and so was Tudor, we got along famously. Many times, he and I would meet at the Oak Room at the Plaza Hotel in New York, and dish everyone. I first met Tudor in London, when we both took class with Marie Rambert, who, like my wife Ariane, had been a pupil of Dalcroze. I was just a student at the time, but I hated Rambert's class. I didn't like the way she taught—for the most part, she avoided the barre. For me, barre work was very important, and I was used to what I had learned from Preobrajenska, Madame Rousanne and Idzikowsky.

I have always been a great admirer of Antony Tudor. His ballets were not only theatrical, they also carried deep psychological meaning and had a purity that made them easy to understand. I admired his ballet *Lilac Garden*, but needless to say, my favorite was *Pillar of Fire*, because Nora Kaye danced the lead. That was a great dramatic role, and today, in my opinion, no one is able to dance it. No, there isn't a dancer who can follow Nora Kaye.

I began to make arrangements to dance with Nora in Japan after she signed a contract with me. We would dance *Giselle* for one month, followed by a month of *Swan Lake*. Shortly before we were to leave, I got a note from Nora from Italy where she was with New York City Ballet, telling me that Balanchine would not give her permission to go to Japan because he needed her. This would not be the last time I got last-minute news like this from Nora, but since it was the first, I panicked. I pleaded with Nora to convince Balanchine to let her leave. I don't know what she said to him, but after a little bit of arm-twisting on her part, he agreed.

Nora and I arrived in Tokyo a month before our first public performance to begin rehearsals with the Komaki. Nora was received as one of America's greatest ballerinas. Photographers snapped our photo as we left the airplane, and we were treated like royalty. She was presented with colorful kimonos and exquisite pearls. We stayed in rooms next to each other at the Imperial Hotel. We performed at the Nichigeti Theater, which was the largest venue for important performances in Japan at the time. It was a round building, and over it hung a huge banner that spilled to the floor: "Nora Kaye and Paul Szilard in *Giselle*."

The local promoter gave a party in our honor to which he invited prominent members of Japanese society. The only problem was that Nora hated Japanese food, so while we were at the hotel getting dressed, we made a deal. Nora would tell everyone that she was on a very strict diet. Whenever a dish of Japanese delicacies would appear before her, she would look at me, ask my permission, and I, in my strictest voice, would say, "Absolutely not."

At the party we were seated on the floor in the traditional Japanese fashion: shoes off, legs twisted underneath our bodies. Nora and I kept elbowing each other as the food was brought in. "Oh, Paul. May I eat that? It looks delicious."

"Absolutely not, Nora."

And she'd look crestfallen, but I knew she was happy to let the octopus, or fugu, the deadly blowfish, pass her by. I had never heard of fugu before, but we were told that if the sushi chef cuts it the wrong way and hits a nerve in the fish, whoever eats it will die within minutes. It was presented to our table on a huge platter, and had been sliced so thin as to be nearly transparent. Each slice was topped with the bright orange roe of the fish. As pretty as it looked, I had no intention of letting raw fish be my last meal.

Things were going according to plan until Nora started to improvise a little too much. When another dish came, and I told her she was not allowed to eat it, she turned to our hosts, and in her own, unique Nora voice said, "Oh, isn't he awful. He won't let me eat a thing and I'm starving."

Now all eyes were on me.

"Nora," I said, "one more crack like that and I am going to give you permission to eat the fugu." I began to raise my hand to signal the waiter.

She took my hand and told our hosts, "He really does take good care of me."

We started work in the Komaki rehearsal studios. Before we left the States, I had told Nora to make sure she brought her costumes, including the wigs.

"Absolutely not, Paul. The Japanese are famous for their costumes, and especially their wigs. I want to order everything when I get there. It will be fabulous."

Well, I really couldn't argue with Nora on that, but it did leave me feeling slightly uncomfortable to arrive without costumes. A few days after we arrived a seamstress was brought to the theater to measure and fit Nora for costumes and wigs for *Giselle*.

One morning, I was in my dressing room getting ready for rehearsal when I heard a piercing scream and then thunderous waves of laughter coming from Nora's dressing room, which was right next door. I rushed from my room into Nora's and found her standing in front of the mirror, with the wigmaker at her feet. Nora was hysterical with laughter. The wigmaker was just hysterical.

Nora looked like a puppet, but more like Medusa than

Petrouchka. The hair of the wig was sticking out like branches in a tree. It never would have worked for the mad scene in *Giselle*, where her hair has to come undone. I doubled over in peals of laughter. Nora's mascara started to run, which only made her look more frightening.

The only person not enjoying this was the young wigmaker, who was in tears. She probably thought she was delivering a masterpiece. Nora and I tried to calm her down. The Japanese are such a proud people, and we didn't mean to hurt her feelings. Nora changed into her everyday clothes, ran out, and bought her a big box of chocolates.

On opening night at the Nichigeti Theatre, Nora and I believed we had given a wonderful performance of *Giselle*. We had worked ourselves into a frenzy, especially Nora, who danced with so much emotional depth and clarity that she would have brought down any house. This night, when the curtain closed, Nora and I both knew we had done something special. The curtain opened, and one, maybe two people in the audience clapped. The rest were silent. We were crestfallen. When the curtain closed again, Nora turned to me and said, in her typical wry way, "Well, honey, we are a flop."

We had no idea at the time that in those days the Japanese simply did not applaud. In their tradition of Noh, Kabuki, and Bunraku, clapping is unheard of. I wish someone would have explained that to us before the performance. Nora and I were ready to pack our bags and head home.

Those winter days in Japan were very cold, but each evening I liked to walk back to the hotel, which was only a few blocks away. I felt I needed to breathe fresh air and unwind a bit after the performance. Many times, I would be stopped by prostitutes, not for solicitations, but for my autograph. "*Paul San*, autograph." Some carried souvenir programs. They had come to see the show. We couldn't get anyone to applaud at the theater, but we were a hit among the prostitutes. I couldn't wait to tell Nora!

There is a part in the second act of the ballet when Giselle floats in from the grave looking rather ethereal. She's come back from the dead to save Albrecht from the fate of the Wilis. Giselle would float onto the stage, then disappear. She'd float in again, then disappear again. One hundred years earlier, when the ballet was originally performed (1841), there was a special device that the ballerina would step into in order to make these quick entrances and departures from the grave. If done correctly, it would look like she was flying. But one night, Nora stepped into the wooden contraption created by the Japanese, and a few people backstage lowered and then raised her. When they did it a second time, the machine got stuck with Nora in the down position. The stagehands could not get her back up. She was screaming through her teeth, "Get me out of this fucking thing." By all accounts, Nora was a most unique Giselle.

One day, we were invited to see the Kabuki from special seats in a private box at the theater. Each box had its own set of curtains. About halfway through the performance, Nora became tired and bored, and her head began to bob and her eyes close. She turned to me and in her best stage whisper said, "Paul, close the curtain."

"Nora, I can't do that. People are watching you. What will they think?"

"Close the curtain. Now!" she said.

And so I closed the curtain just enough to cover Nora, who then fell fast asleep. Good thing she didn't snore.

When the month of *Giselles* was over, it was time for a month of *Swan Lake*. We still hadn't seen Nora's costumes for this role, even when we had already begun dress rehearsals. Because of our experience with *Giselle*, we were a bit nervous. Nobody wanted to see Medusa again.

On opening night, when we were onstage getting ready to perform the ballet, I looked around, but there was no Nora. The lights were beginning to dim. All the other dancers were warming up: some at the barre that had been placed in the wings, some stretching and exercising on the floor, others practicing with their partners. Finally Nora came out of the wings, and everybody turned to see her as she walked on stage. So far, so good.

But when I started to try my pirouette with her, I couldn't get near her. Metal rods had been sewn into her tutu to make it extend, but if I approached her from the front, the dress sprung up from the back. And if I tried to lift her from the back, the dress sprung up in the front. She looked like a kewpie doll.

"Somebody get me a scissors," I screamed, and a dresser ran on stage carrying a pair of scissors.

"Paul, are you crazy?" Nora asked.

"Nora. Trust me on this. We have no choice."

I began to cut the tutu and the metal fell to the floor. When I was finished, the tutu behaved and lay straight against Nora's body.

"Look at me. I look like I just got out of the shower," she said. The tutu was completely flat and limp.

I remember entering her hotel room in Tokyo the evening we were going to a fancy party. She needed a few more minutes to get ready, and as I waited and looked down at her bed, I couldn't believe all the fabulous jewelry she had.

"Nora," I called out, "are these faux or are they real?"

"Darling, they're real. Harry Winston."

I didn't give it much more thought until a few months later, when we were back in the United States. I picked up one of the newspapers, and there was a picture of Nora. I read the article and learned that the man who had given Nora all her jewelry had yet to pay for it. And now Harry Winston was demanding that his gems be returned.

Nora refused.

She was taken to court and was forced to return all the jewelry.

I called Nora on the phone and asked what happened. "Well, my dear," she said, "I fucked for nothing."

It was extraordinary to work with Nora because she was such a wonderful performer. When you rehearsed a ballet with Nora, she believed that everything had to be danced to its fullest. There was never any marking steps with her. She did everything on toe, when other dancers go on half-toe during rehearsals.

I choreographed a ballet for her, a *pas de deux*, called *Night Fright*, with music by Ravel, *Le Tombeau de Couperin*. We danced it in Tokyo for the first time. Nora was a much more important, much more famous dancer than I. To work with such a partner can be intimidating. When I choreographed, there would be times steps would not come easy. Many dancers lose their patience during these "down" moments, and their annoyance breaks the creative flow. But not Nora. She was always encouraging, and often said, "Paul, relax. Think about what you want and it will come."

When you dance, there are certain things that cannot be learned, that have to come from inside you. To the steps you add who you are and what you feel. Even though we had set choreography, especially in *Giselle* and *Swan Lake*, sometimes the feeling would change. Not the steps, but the feeling. Nora and I clicked perfectly together.

There was always something new with Nora on stage, because she would always add something artistically to her performance. I was constantly surprised by the freshness she brought to a role. There are many aspects of dance which are not found in the choreography, but in the feeling, expression, and delivery. Her gift was not just in doing the steps, but what she brought to the steps.

She had a very strong technique, and was very dramatic. Her body was a little bit stocky, and her legs were not extremely long. Nevertheless, whatever she did was extremely effective.

When we returned to the United States, Nora wanted ABT to pick up my ballet, *Night Fright*. She met with Lucia Chase, director of the company, to see what could be done. Nora and I danced it for Lucia who became very interested. It was decided that Nora would dance *Night Fright* with Johnny Kriza, a star of ABT. Everything was going according to plan until Lucia learned what the royalty would be for the Ravel score, and what the orchestra would cost. Then she said she could not afford these expenses. Lucia was *very* economical. And the whole project fell apart.

Nora and I always remained close friends. When you're a friend of Nora, you feel completely free. That means I could tell her stories from my private life. Not only what happened during the day . . . but what happened at night as well. She adored listening to it, dirt and all. And she was the same way with me, very open about both her private and professional lives. This always brought us close together.

When she married Herbert Ross and they were working on their film *Nijinsky*, she contacted me because many important parts of Nijinsky's life took place in Budapest. She and Herb wanted to rent the Budapest Opera House, and I put Nora in touch with the right people in Hungary. I was in Paris at the time. Later, she and Herb went to Bari, Italy, to film *Giselle* with Baryshnikov, Alexandra Ferri, Leslie Browne, and Carla Fracci. She said, "Come to Bari." I said, "No." She said, "Please come to Bari. I haven't seen you in such a long time. Come. We will have a good laugh." At that time, Nora was already sick, so I decided to go. At rehearsals, at the Bari Opera House, she was in pretty bad shape, sitting with a nurse who traveled with her. I was glad I went because a few months later I got the news that she had passed away. That was a very sad day for me.

A Few Thoughts on Dance

I don't believe a choreographer should rework a classical ballet, such as *Giselle* or *Swan Lake*. Today, though choreographers follow the basic structure of the original, they add to it and change it, which I am absolutely against. Today, we see productions with new choreography of *Swan Lake*, *Giselle*, and *Sleeping Beauty*. But I have to ask myself, what for? You don't change the composition of Chopin or Stravinsky, so why change the composition of the standard, traditional ballet we're accustomed to?

Why do we have to change *Swan Lake* when it's been around for more than one hundred years? Why does a young choreographer think he can do it better? I don't believe he can. If choreographers don't agree with or respect the original, they shouldn't touch it. Why not do a new *Giselle* of their own choreography?

That's one reason why I'm a great admirer of Jerry Robbins. He made a ballet of *Afternoon of a Faun*, the famous Nijinsky ballet, which has nothing to do with the original. The idea is the same, the feeling is the same, but it's an entirely new conception. Clearly, there's room for new choreography, like Matthew Bourne's recent *Swan Lake*. I accepted that, though I did not find the ballet entirely successful. I thought that Bourne's use of male dancers was wrong. I would have preferred it as a real *travestie*—something to laugh about rather than having to take so seriously.

Romola Nijinsky

I always thought of Romola Nijinsky as a latter-day Lucrezia Borgia—you'd turn your back for a second and the dazzling ring would open and the poison would fill the glass. Romola was a bitch, but a fabulous bitch, and a very great woman. She had a deep love of the dance, and respected the fact that I had been a dancer. But she also used me. Her dirty work always had to be done by somebody else.

Romola herself told me she was never on good terms with anyone from the Nijinsky family. She was the daughter of the famous Hungarian actress Emilia Markus, whom I saw on stage when I was a young boy in Budapest. Her voice was deep and overly dramatic, and when she appeared, your focus immediately was on her. She carried herself like a queen. Though she was already old by then, she was still playing young women like Shakespeare's Juliet. Markus had the same reputation in the theater as Eleonora Duse or Sarah Bernhardt: these women were the undisputed stars of the time.

Romola Nijinsky, *née* de Pulszky, was the daughter of a grand and admired lady, who very much objected to Romola's marriage to Vaslav Nijinsky because as a dancer he was considered way below her station. After they were married, Romola told me that

Emilia Markus referred to her son-in-law as a hoofer. Markus, whose repertoire was classical, from Shakespeare to Chekhov, felt there was a huge difference between what she did on the stage and what Vaslav did. She acted; he hoofed.

Romola and Nijinsky had two daughters, Kyra and Tamara. Tamara became an actress, and later emigrated to Canada. Rumors started to spread that Tamara was not the daughter of Nijinsky, as he had been in a sanitarium for more than a year before her birth. The dates just didn't add up. But Romola told me that Tamara was indeed his child, and that while Vaslav was hospitalized, his doctor suggested sex might help his condition. Romola insisted that Tamara was conceived during a conjugal visit to the sanitarium. Who knows if this is true?

When Romola talked with me about her private life, she admitted to me she was lesbian and had a girlfriend in Japan, in the all-female Takarazuka Troupe, which is known all over the world as a theatrical group where the male parts are performed by women. I had the opportunity to meet the girlfriend once; she was a beautiful woman. Romola was desperately in love with her, went to Tokyo to visit, and lavished presents on her, including a mink stole. Romola and I spent one New Year's Eve together in Tokyo at the Imperial Hotel. This was before Japan was completely westernized, and when you stepped outside the door of your hotel at night, people came up to you wanting to know if there was anything they could do for you sexually. As it was New Year's, Romola and I were in the mood for a little adventure, so she grabbed my arm and said, "Let's do something exciting." After we left the hotel, we let one man follow us for about a block. He whispered something, but it was hard to understand him.

"Do you want to see sex with a woman?" he asked in his best English.

"No," I said, "doesn't interest me."

"With a boy?"

"No."

"How about two women together?"

"That's it," Romola said. "Oh, this is terribly exciting."

It was very dark and very late and the three of us got into a taxi and headed out to God knows where. We kept driving in the countryside: by now it was nearly two in the morning, and Romola started to panic. "They're going to kill us!" she whispered in my ear, and then, piece by piece, she removed her jewelry and hid it. Soon after, the taxi came to a stop. We had arrived at a traditional Japanese house in the woods. A few flakes of snow started falling, but melted as soon as they touched our woolen coats. Freezing cold, we were greeted by a very polite woman in a red kimono. We removed our shoes and were seated on a long, narrow couch. At this point, Romola put her earrings back on, wanting to look as glamorous as possible for our hostess.

A few minutes later, two young women entered the room, one carrying a tatami mat, which she unfolded on the floor, as well as a box of kleenex. They undressed, and began to have sex in front of us—their sleek bodies writhing. Romola, who was so excited by this, turned to me and said, "This is the greatest choreography I ever saw."

On our way out, she pointed to the dildo they carried and said, "You must get me one of those!"

"OK, OK, I'll try."

I went to our guide and asked him where we could buy a dildo. As it was 2 A.M., he said that all the shops he knew of were of course closed, but if we liked, we could have the one they had just used. He offered to put a condom on it, to make it clean. So I bought it.

After Japan, we'd see each other all the time in New York. Romola had a tiny one-bedroom apartment on Fifth Avenue. I never knew how she supported herself. There were rumors about inheritances and money in foreign banks. But since she was smart, distinguished, and knew how to wear good clothes, she looked proper, even without the money. Somehow, she and her companion, Baron Bohus, managed to travel everywhere. Bohus, like a member of the family, functioned as personal promoter, cook, secretary, and washing lady. He and Romola mingled with high society, which welcomed them because everyone was interested in Vaslav Nijinsky. And Bohus, very clever in maintaining their social circle, saw to it that they were constantly invited to exclusive parties on Park Avenue. I heard that Romola was able to borrow money from these people, a little at a time, but by always having Bohus to do the negotiating, she kept her hands clean.

Romola always played the grand dame as she searched for investors to back her projects: a new book, a new film, a new idea. One day she said to me, "Paul, I need a new typewriter. Get me one."

"How?" I asked, knowing she was up to something.

"Well, why don't you go to the Italian typewriter company, Olivetti, and tell them that if I get a typewriter I will write my next book with it. They can use my name in publicity."

I called Olivetti, and they agreed to give Romola a typewriter. La Borgia had struck again!

Once, when she didn't have a place to stay in New York, I arranged for her to use my friend Anton Dolin's apartment while he was away. When he returned, he called me at once. "Paul, that bitch has stolen all of my linens!"

Over the years several people wanted to make a film with Romola about Nijinsky, but nothing ever panned out. Each time, however, she was paid handsomely for the option to the story, and she made a fair amount of money that way. Alexander Korda bought it the first time, but he had so many problems with Romola he gave up on the project, allowing her to sell the rights again. Even the great director King Vidor bought an option from her, only to let it run out, whereupon Romola and her story were back on the market. Most of the interest in the material was rooted in the relationship between Nijinsky and Serge Diaghilev—their love affair. But in those days, homosexuality didn't play well in the movies; in fact, on the surface it was nonexistent. Filmmakers could not find an acceptable way to weave this material into the story, and, without it, their scripts didn't make sense.

Sometimes Romola's endless supply of ideas included me. Because we both needed money, she and I did some lecture demonstrations. She would tell stories about Vaslav, both professional and personal, while I performed my own choreography—and nobody knew the difference between mine and Nijinsky's. Romola could say unbelievable things about Nijinsky's talent when prompted to by the members of the audience.

"Tell me, Madame Nijinsky, how far could Nijinsky jump?" one person asked.

Then Romola looked around the theater and came up with something unbelievable: "I'd say my Vaslav could jump from where you're sitting in the audience to where Mr. Szilard and I are onstage." That was quite a distance. I was furious and embarrassed.

I remember leaving the theater and finding a few people waiting at the stage door for an autograph because they thought I was Nijinsky.

"Oh, Mr. Nijinsky, please give us your autograph." The first time I heard that, I was stunned. I couldn't believe that they thought I was Nijinsky. But to make them happy, I took a pen and signed their programs "Vaslav Nijinsky."

Romola was furious when she saw this. "How dare you sign Vaslav's name?" she yelled.

"Romola," I answered, "if these people want to get an autograph from Nijinsky, then why shouldn't I make them happy." I made everyone happy, except for Romola, who was fuming. Eventually, she cooled off and gave me a worn-out, broken-down pair of ballet shoes that she swore were Nijinsky's. I doubted it.

Romola recalled the time Nijinsky was let out of the asylum and they were living outside of London. When he wanted to see the Royal Ballet, he would be taken to Covent Garden and given seats in a box. Evidently, at one of the performances, a leading ballerina was a bit overweight, and Nijinsky got so enraged and verbally abusive that he had to be removed from the theater. He could not stand fat people.

Romola told me that Nijinsky liked to have tea at the Dorchester Hotel, which was the place for high tea in those days. Unfortunately, one afternoon a fat woman walked in and passed Nijinsky, which got him so agitated that he took the cushion from a chair and threw it at her. They had to take him home immediately.

Kyra Nijinsky

While I was teaching at Ballet Arts in New York City, Romola asked me to help bring her daughter Kyra to the United States because she was in a precarious financial position back in Italy. Lord knows what else was going wrong with Kyra at the time. I looked everywhere for a sponsor, and finally got Ballet Arts, at Carnegie Hall, to offer her a teaching position. When she arrived and began her work, she became one of the most unpopular teachers Ballet Arts had ever hired. Enrollment plummeted. She had her own ideas about ballet and how to teach it, which had nothing to do with what was then considered traditional, appropriate, or correct. It wasn't long before she was fired and she moved out to California, where her aunt, the great choreographer Bronislava Nijinska, Vaslav's sister, was teaching.

As a young woman, Kyra had been a dancer, and when I was still in Budapest, she performed in concert, often dancing the male roles. She had very heavy legs, was strong as an ox, and looked like a man. A stocky woman, she carried her weight like a peasant. She married the famous conductor Igor Markevitch. I asked Romola all the time, "How is it possible that Markevitch and Kyra married?" Romola replied that she never understood why he married Kyra since it was rumored at the time that Markevitch was one of the boyfriends of Diaghilev.

Many years later, in San Francisco, Kyra made a very interesting film about Nijinsky, her father, *She Dances Alone*, with Patrick Dupond, a star of the Paris Opera Ballet, who was, and still is, under my management. I don't think Kyra knew her father as well as she claimed, because she was just a young girl when he entered the asylum. Nevertheless, in the movie, she tells stories about her father, while Patrick brought Nijinsky's roles to life on the screen, one by one, as they were mentioned. "When my father danced in

Giselle . . ." she began in her thick, Hungarian accent, and the camera would focus on Patrick as Nijinsky's Albrecht. In addition to *Giselle*, the other ballets in the film included Fokine's *Polovetzian Dances from Prince Igor*, *Spectre de la Rose*, and *Petrouchka*.

I hadn't seen Kyra since she had left New York many years before, so the first time we met in San Francisco, she screamed and we ran to each other and kissed in the Hungarian way. The first morning of rehearsal for the film, Kyra seemed rather bewildered and asked, "Who is this Patrick Dupond? I've never heard of him. Tell him to dance something for me." Patrick was surprised that she had never heard of him. He was, after all, a star.

As he started to dance, you could see Kyra's eyes grow wider and wider, until at last she ran over to Patrick in a hysterical fit. "This . . ." she said, practically falling to her knees, ". . . this boy is the reincarnation of my Vaslav." She became nearly unhinged, like someone who believes she's just found God. Even her hair seemed electrified.

"Darling," she said to Patrick, "you are the greatest!"

As the rehearsal days went on, Kyra began to tell Patrick how to perform, approaching him with instructions and corrections she should have left behind in Carnegie Hall, if not Hungary. She worked Patrick up into a fury, until he finally ran to me and said, "Paul, I don't know what to do with this crazy woman. She wants to tell *me* how to dance, but it's not ballet. She twisted me in such a way I almost fell on my ass with her seventh position."

I finally went to Kyra to try and save the situation, which was getting hotter and hotter on both sides. I said to her in Hungarian, "Kyra, you are just so wonderful, but what you are doing is too much for one person. Let's divide the work. I will help to stage *Giselle* and *Spectre de la Rose*, because I danced them so many times myself and I know the choreography. You stage the other two ballets because I never danced them."

"Oh, Paul," she said, "that is a wonderful idea."

She turned to the director and members of the crew and said, "Ladies and gentlemen, my greatest friend, Paul Szilard, is going to take over the rehearsals of *Giselle* and *Spectre*, because it is too much for me."

Kyra would be summoned to work with a polite "Miss Nijinsky, will you please come on stage." She'd try to begin speaking her lines, but inevitably she became distracted by some slight disturbance and burst into a small fit. She insisted on complete silence in the studio. "Stop it. Stop it," she'd say, "I cannot do this unless there is silence." Once she placed her hand above her eyes, looked out to see an unfamiliar face, and demanded that the one who was talking be thrown out. "Who is she?" Kyra demanded to know.

I rushed to the stage and said, "Kyra, what have you done? That woman you just threw out is one of the backers."

"Oh my God," she said, "Get her back immediately!"

Kyra's reputation for eccentricity was strongly enhanced by her religious faith. Each morning she arrived on the set with her Catholic priest. They both wore black, head to toe, and walked very slowly. Every time she was called onto the sound stage to speak her lines, the priest had to give his blessing in order for Kyra to begin. While this was happening, no one was allowed to speak or to move. And whenever someone yelled "Cut," she ran back for another blessing.

So much for my days in San Francisco. At night, I had to keep an eye on Patrick because he went out to the clubs and bars and returned to the hotel with barely any time to sleep before he was due back on the set. A car would come to pick him up each morning at six, and he needed to wake up an hour earlier. It was my job to wake him. One morning, I barely got him ready and into the car. I returned to my own room, and about an hour later the phone rang. It was Patrick. "Paul, I forgot my costume."

I went back to his room, which was in a state of disarray, and finally found the costume, balled up and soaking wet from perspiration, underneath a pile of other clothes. I had borrowed the costume, which was made after the original by the great designer Léon Bakst, from the Paris Opera Ballet, with my assurance that I'd take good care of it—after all, it was something of a treasure. And now, below me was this inside-out, kind of smelly rag. I had to dig it out like an archaeologist, bring it down to the lobby, and wait for the car that was sent to pick it up.

In spite of such crises, *She Dances Alone* proved a huge success and won an award at the Cannes Film Festival. It was financed by Earle Mack, a well-known patron of the arts. Kyra and I remained friends for a time, but eventually drifted apart. In later years I talked to her a couple of times, and sometimes I'd send her a little money, but I never got to see her before she passed away in 1998.

The Paul Szilard Dance Company

After my success as a dancer in Japan, many people approached me to organize a company under my own name. In 1954, when the Meinichi newspaper agreed to sponsor it, I accepted, and began to work on putting together a company and a repertory. I decided that the *The Miraculous Mandarin*, danced to one of Bartok's most famous scores, would be the centerpiece, with myself in the role of the Mandarin. It had been choreographed by Gyula Harangozó in Budapest in 1945. The libretto was by Melchior Lengyel, the great Hungarian writer, but I found some parts unimportant and had a few ideas about making the libretto more contemporary. In New York, where we both were living then, I told Lengyel what I had in mind for the ballet, and he agreed and reconceived it for me.

Later, I engaged Colette Marchand from Paris as principal dancer. Colette was a leading dancer in Ballets de Paris de Roland Petit, and was the star of the John Huston film about Henri de Toulouse-Lautrec, *Moulin Rouge*. She was one of the most distinguished dancers I had ever worked with—polite, well-educated, and beautiful. She was famous for her long, statuesque legs. For the Japanese tour, I insured her legs for one million dollars, not just for publicity reasons (though that was part of it) but also in case something really did happen to them.

I also engaged Milorad Miskovitch, a wonderful dancer from

Yugoslavia, as famous in Europe as Colette was. I signed on another twenty-five or so dancers, some formerly with ABT and other companies. It took us over thirty hours to arrive in Japan by propeller plane, changing planes four times. By the time we got to Tokyo, we were completely worn out as we were greeted enthusiastically at the airport and given flowers and kimonos. Photographers and journalists asked us questions like "Do you like Japan?" though our feet had barely touched the ground.

All we wanted to do then was go to the hotel and pee. (I always had the same room in the Imperial Hotel, which was built by Frank Lloyd Wright, room 325.) Instead, as good guests we had no choice but to follow the protocol devised by our hosts. Colette, Miskovitch, and I sat in an open car for the three-hour trip while the driver played the hit theme song from the movie *Moulin Rouge*—repeatedly. We almost died. At that time, the trip from the airport to the city passed through farmlands and peasant towns. People would stand at the side of the road and stare at our entourage as it made its way to Tokyo. Once in a while somebody would wave, but for the most part we were regarded as visitors from another planet. Actually, nobody had any idea who the hell we were and why we were playing that horrible music.

When we got down to work, soon after our arrival, in addition to *Mandarin*, I choreographed a short ballet for Colette and Miskovitch, *Salome*, with music from the opera by Richard Strauss. The ballet programs and the company achieved great success and we were asked to return to Japan. I decided, however, that running a ballet company was too difficult and too expensive. I just did not have the money for it, and we disbanded when we finished the tour.

Nemchinova's Leg

Madame Nemchinova was as brilliant a dancer as Danilova—they were the prima ballerinas in the days of the Diaghilev ballet. Nemchinova was a strong technician, but she never had the same success in America as Alexandra Danilova. Born in Russia in 1899,

Madame became a member of Diaghilev's Ballets Russes, where Bronislava Nijinska choreographed *Les Biches* for her in 1924.

One thing I've noticed while studying and working with Russian dancers is that they always speak very possessively of their roles: "It's my ballet. My ballet." Years after they stop dancing, it's still "my ballet." And when they can barely walk anymore, it's still "my ballet."

When the Marquis de Cuevas's company came to the United States and danced at Carnegie Hall, with Danilova performing the lead in *Les Biches*, Nemchinova invited me to go with her to see the performance. As Nemchinova and I settled into our seats, she began to speak of "my ballet." "This is my ballet, my ballet, and nobody even thought about inviting me to a rehearsal. Absolutely not. They forget about me." She felt she had been thoroughly slighted.

Finally, when the performance started and Danilova danced, Nemchinova turned to me, her right hand pointing to her left palm at about a forty-five degree angle. She made a face and, like a woodpecker, repeated her hand gesture a couple of times. According to Nemchinova, Danilova did not have a good instep, and did not have a straight, classical line.

One of the joys of my dancing days was taking class from Nemchinova, though she never attracted very many pupils and would often come to class a little tipsy. I was one of her regulars, as was Jerry Robbins. She was not a clever woman, but she had the sense to tell you why you could not do a certain step and a stunning ability to find a dancer's faults and straighten them out. She liked me very much. For a time, I had a problem with pirouettes, and she had a dynamic way of making corrections—showing me exactly what I was doing wrong and how I could make it better. That was her gift. Nevertheless, she was not popular as a teacher and sometimes there'd be only three or four of us in her class.

Occasionally, I'd take classes with her husband, Anatole Oboukhov, who was a premier danseur at the Maryinsky, and partnered Anna Pavlova in her final performances in Russia in

1914. When I knew him, he was a teacher at the School of American Ballet in New York City. He was famous for having the most important men's class. He was a dancer in the grand Russian style, and quite an elegant man. He was already in his fifties when I studied with him, and still had such a commanding personality that no one moved when he faced you. "One. Two. Three. Plié," he'd begin class, sharply and crisply. He was famous for standing in front of a dancer and snapping his fingers while he counted the beat. Though he would never say your name, he would look you right in the eye, an inch from your face, and say "Mister, Mister," in time with the movement, while we practically froze with fear.

One day Nemchinova came to see me at the SAB studio because she had found out I was going to sail to Europe shortly for Easter on one of my frequent trips there.

"Paul," she said, "when you go to Europe, you have to do me a great favor."

"Yes, of course. What is it?"

"We have some gifts that we want to send to Madame Egorova." Lubov Egorova had been a major star in the Russian Imperial ballet, and Diaghilev's Ballets Russes, and was one of the top teachers in Paris since opening her studio there in 1923.

Nemchinova asked me to come to her and Oboukhov's apartment in New York City to pick up the gifts. When I went there a few days before my trip, the door opened on a dining room table stacked with presents, among them a whole cooked ham. There were also packages of chewing gum for the children and grandchildren, as well as pound after pound of chocolate. I almost died when I saw how much she expected me to carry. I didn't know where I'd put it all, or if customs would even let me in.

As I did not dare to refuse, I took it all with me and brought it to my apartment. But instead of carrying it to France, I left the gifts all behind. When I arrived in Paris, I went to the markets and bought a cooked ham, chewing gum, and pound after pound of dark chocolate and brought it to Madame Egorova's studio.

Before I returned home, Madame Egorova asked me to bring

95

something back to Nemchinova. Another favor! It was a small statue, cast in plaster, of Nemchinova's leg en pointe. When I arrived at customs in New York, the customs people could not believe what I was carrying. Indeed, they took it away from me for a short time and drilled a hole in it to see what I was smuggling into the States. I left the airport with my three legs intact, and brought the statue to Nemchinova. When she opened the door to her apartment, she was simply delighted to have her leg back.

PART III

MR. B AND NEW YORK CITY BALLET

New York City Ballet

M Y FIRST REAL SUCCESS HAD BEEN AS A DANCER and an im-presario in Japan. As a result, I was well known there, and in 1958, the NHK, the most important radio and TV conglomerate in Japan, asked if I could bring the New York City Ballet to their country. When I returned to New York I went to see Balanchine and Lincoln Kirstein, the co-founders of New York City Ballet, and Betty Cage, the general manager. They were very interested in my proposition, and agreed to work with me. It was amazing that a little-known impresario could sign a contract with the biggest dance company in the world. After all, I was not a household name, like Sol Hurok, the leading impresario of the time.

New York City Ballet had always been a dream of mine. I adored George Balanchine and his ballets and regarded him as the greatest innovator in the dance of the last century. I wanted to get close to this company, and thought being an impresario would be my way to achieve this. I was thrilled to be invited to rehearsals and performances, and to see the stars of those days: Maria Tallchief, Nora Kaye, André Eglevsky, and the rest. At the time, New York City Ballet was not as popular abroad as it is today. Now, they are considered *the* company of America, but in those days they were looked upon as experimental theater.

I negotiated a six-month tour for the City Ballet, underwritten by the U.S. State Department, for performances in Japan, Australia, and the Philippines. The company would dance in Tokyo, Osaka, Sydney, Melbourne, and Manila. After the tour was over, I was established as a specialist in the countries of the Pacific. Everybody who wanted to go there wanted to come with me.

Maria Tallchief and André Eglevsky were the stars of the company and received special billing for their performances. Maria, the former Mrs. George Balanchine, was the Oklahoma-born ballerina who became one of the most famous dancers in the world. Her sister, Marjorie, too, was a wonderful dancer. Eglevsky, Russian-born, had joined New York City Ballet in 1951, and proceeded to dazzle audiences with his bravura style.

When the contracts for the tour were signed, with the names Tallchief and Eglevsky in bold letters, and all the travel plans made, Maria came to me and said that she didn't want to go to Japan. And then, of course, Eglevsky came to me and said, "If she doesn't go, then I don't go. What would be the point?"

I was beside myself. I must have talked to Maria a hundred times, begging her to change her mind. I desperately needed her on this tour in order to make it a hit. Finally, after some arm-twisting on my part, she said, "All right, Paul. I will come to Japan, but for only one week and then I'm coming home."

"Fine." I would have accepted anything at this point.

Then I went to Eglevsky, who said, "Why should I bother going to Japan at all, if she's coming right back. And besides, Balanchine hates me."

"André, you are being silly. Why should Mr. B hate you?"

"I don't know. He just hates me."

I went to Mr. B, explained the situation, and reminded him that we had a signed contract for a six-month tour. Without Maria and André the whole thing would fall apart. Their names were already printed on the posters.

I said to Mr. B, "Can you talk to André? He feels that you are not interested in him."

Balanchine refused at first. Many times I went backstage at City Center, where the New York City Ballet then performed, to see Balanchine: he would wince a bit and say, "Not today, not today."

One day I just looked at him and he said, "OK, OK." He must have sensed my desperation, and during intermission, we both made our way upstairs to André's dressing room. Mr. B went inside and I stayed out.

In a short time the door flew open, Balanchine walked out, and I went in to talk to André. He was sitting at the makeup table, preparing for the next ballet.

"Well, what happened? What did he say?" I asked.

He turned to look at me and, raising one eyebrow, said, "Balanchine told me how awful I danced tonight."

I couldn't believe it! I had finally persuaded Mr. B to talk to him, and this was the outcome.

"André," I said, "what do you want him to do, go down on his knees?"

No response.

"André, he came up to see you, he talked to you. Regardless of his opinion of how you danced tonight, Mr. B still spoke to you. He's trying."

Finally, André agreed to come on tour. Reluctantly. But he agreed.

Then, another problem popped up. When I was negotiating with the Japanese and deciding on repertory, they insisted that City Ballet come with *Swan Lake*. In my experiences with the Japanese, you have to come to them with either *Swan Lake* or *Giselle*. Anything else is not really interesting to them. I told the manager of the Japanese theater that, unfortunately, New York City Ballet has no three-act *Swan Lake*. They have a one-act version of the ballet choreographed by Balanchine. The negotiations went on for many months because the Japanese insisted on the traditional *Swan Lake*. It reached a point where I had to tell them that if they wanted a full-length *Swan Lake*, then they should bring in another company. Finally, after enormous effort on my part, they agreed to the program the New York City Ballet had offered.

We left for Japan from New York on a Pan Am clipper, the Concorde of its day (a very slow Concorde). The plane had two levels. On the main level were the regular passenger seats, with about four or five sleeping berths. To decide which dancers could sleep first, we put everybody's name in a hat and chose six of them. These dancers got to sleep for about three hours, at which point out came the hat and we chose new names. The next day, after thirty-two hours and four stop-overs, we arrived in Japan.

One of the first things I did when I got to the theater was to take a look at the printed program. It was a beautiful book, but when I opened it, I saw "Full-Length *Swan Lake*." I was thunderstruck. After all I had told them, they had still put it in. They thought by doing this that somehow we'd come up with a three-act *Swan Lake*. I ran to the manager and told him that if they did not reprint the entire program, we would not perform. The next day, there was a completely new program. It featured all the dancers, principals and members of the corps, with one very important exception: André Eglevsky! I was sure that if André saw this, he would be on the next plane home. The only thing that could be done was to print copies of André's photo and insert them into all the programs.

Tokyo seemed like a welcoming venue for the City Ballet, and I arranged for some publicity through an American journalist from a Japanese-American newspaper. Each week he interviewed a different star from the company, including Maria Tallchief, Melissa Hayden, and André Eglevsky.

A few days after the Eglevsky interview I was having tea in the hotel when I read the headline: *"One of the world's greatest dancers from the New York City Ballet says that all male dancers are homosexual."*

It wasn't long before I felt the effects of that, mildly speaking, faux pas. Lincoln Kirstein, co-director of City Ballet, became hysterical and held me responsible for any repercussions since I had given the journalist permission to interview the dancers. "How dare this man write this," he shouted.

"Lincoln, I can't control what he writes in the paper. I will speak to him and see what I can do." I was trying my best to smooth things out, but I was angry, too. In those days, that kind of publicity could sink careers.

I asked the journalist to come to the Imperial Hotel, where three of us—Lincoln, a male dancer from City Ballet, and I—were waiting for him. The first ten seconds of our meeting were very polite, but it was obvious that Lincoln couldn't contain his emotions very long before they exploded. "Aren't you ashamed?" he asked the journalist, "You know this is an American company. How can you write that when you know we were sponsored by the State Department?" This was the period right after Senator McCarthy and the communist witch hunts, and you couldn't even mention the word "homosexual" without causing a scandal.

The journalist was already losing patience and blurted out, "Well, is it true what Eglevsky said?"

"Yes, it's true," Lincoln yelled, "Because all the male dancers in the New York City Ballet get up each morning and suck cock." And then he turned and walked away. The three of us stood there silent. What could you say after that? Only that the Japanese headline didn't sink anyone's career.

Maria was received in Tokyo like a queen. The Japanese went wild over her, giving her pearls, brightly colored kimonos, and many other gifts. Japanese balletomanes had eagerly waited for her arrival at the airport, and Maria, I believe, relished all the attention bestowed on her after that. In fact, she was in heaven, and after her opening night success, she decided to stay longer than the week she had promised me. Soon, we were up to two weeks. Maria ended up staying in Tokyo for the entire four-week engagement, and then came with us to Osaka. I couldn't have been happier. But the morning of opening night in Osaka, I came down to the lobby of the hotel and found Maria in front of me, standing with all of her luggage.

"Maria" I said, "Where are you going?"

"I'm going home. Home. Buzz is waiting for me." Buzz was her husband.

"But, Maria . . ."

She put her hand out and stopped me from saying another

word. "Paul, I told you one week. Look how many weeks I stayed. Please don't continue."

"OK, Maria, you are right."

I had no choice but to accept her decision. As a matter of fact, I went out and bought some flowers for her, and I wished her all the best. Of course, when André learned that Maria was leaving, he wanted to leave, too. After a while, fortunately, he calmed down and agreed to stay a little longer, though he threatened not to come to Sydney or Melbourne.

Now that Maria was gone, what was I going to tell the Australians? On the plane to Sydney, I looked to Betty Cage for advice, only to learn that I was pretty much on my own. "Paul, you are the impresario. Whatever you tell them is your business," she said, trying not to laugh too much.

I decided there was only one way out of this. I was going to have to lie. When we landed in Sydney, we were greeted by the press, and all they were concerned about was Maria and André. Well, André was right next to me. Where was Maria? The press wanted to know.

"I am so sorry," I said, "but Miss Tallchief could not come because . . . well . . . because she is pregnant."

I had no idea where that came from, but oddly enough, I learned later it was true. Maria must have been in the very early stage of pregnancy and had been told by her doctors that she needed to come home and rest.

Our first morning in Sydney, I picked up the newspaper in the hotel lobby and read the headline: "World Famous Ballet Company Arrives Without Its Star." I wanted to buy every copy of that paper and tear it up. It was the first signal of impending disaster. Ticket sales went kaput. Nobody wanted to come. Both the public and the critics in Sydney hated the repertoire because it was too modern for them. In those days in Australia, if you didn't have white feathers on your head, it wasn't considered dance.

Mr. B permitted the company to dance the one-act *Swan Lake* no more than four times in Australia. But ticket sales were so bad that Sir Frank Tate, the director of the theater, begged me to get more *Swan Lake* into the schedule. Sir Frank Tate was a most distinguished gentleman, and very English. He was a very famous theatrical promoter, akin to the Brothers Shubert in America. His office was filled with dark brown leather and heavy furniture. Betty and I called Balanchine in New York and relayed Sir Frank's request. Mr. B said, "Absolutely not. If they don't like our repertoire, it is just too bad. So they shouldn't take us back anymore. We have a reason for being there and that is to show them what we are doing. If they don't like it, tough."

On top of that, since the State Department paid for everything, the Australians couldn't complain that they were losing money. All the same, it was very bad. One night I went to see my old friend Bobby Helpmann, former star of the Royal Ballet, who was now acting in a play a few blocks away from where we were performing. His play was a flop, too.

I went to his dressing room and asked, "How did it go tonight?"

"Wonderful," he said, "At least a hundred people. How about you?"

"About the same."

Balanchine adored Diana Adams, and she was cast as the lead in *Swan Lake*. I had great respect for her because she was one of the most lyrical dancers I ever saw. Even today, I know hardly anyone who can dance the second movement in *Symphony in C* the way she could. I understood why Balanchine had a special feeling for her. I frequently expressed to Diana my admiration for her dancing. As we became friends, we would meet socially, outside the theater. Sadly, she died much too young.

During one rehearsal in Japan, Diana twisted her ankle and had to be replaced. Melissa Hayden, another leading ballerina, was sure that she would be asked to fill in for Diana. Rumor had it that she was already practicing the role. But Betty and I had to call Balanchine back in New York to find out who he wanted cast in the ballet.

"Can Melissa take over the part?" Betty asked.

"Absolutely not. I want somebody else," said Balanchine.

"Then who do you want to put in?"

"Allegra Kent."

That was the first time Allegra was cast in a leading role. Even today, when I run into Allegra at the theater, we talk about those early days in Japan, and her triumph in *Swan Lake*.

Allegra was fantastic. I'll never forget when, later on, she got the lead in Balanchine's *The Seven Deadly Sins*, the music of which was composed by Kurt Weill and sung onstage by his wife Lotte Lenya. Lenya never had a big voice, and as opening night approached, she caught a cold and sounded really awful. The voice was gone, and Lincoln Kirstein was running around the theater saying, "This is going to be a disaster." He told me that if she sang like this the premiere would be ruined. Luckily, there was a miracle, and she got back what she never had!

During dress rehearsal, Allegra looked out of this world. She was the most beautiful creature and the most sexy-looking woman I had ever seen. Allegra also had an unusual quality in her movement which immediately established her as one of the outstanding ballerinas of her day, and a sensuous Broadway star.

The other Balanchine ballet on which Allegra left her mark was *La Somnambule*, also known as *Night Shadow*. I've seen the ballet danced by many ballerinas, but Allegra was the best. It was as if she were floating instead of dancing. Her performances were unforgettable.

There was not much to do in Australia. The dancers would sleep during the day and perform in the evenings. We stayed in apartments, rather than hotels, because of the length of the engagement. But during that cold, bleak winter, most of the apartments, with their primitive, coin-operated heaters, were not very pleasant. However, I had a fairly good apartment with electric heat and hot water that many of the dancers would visit to take showers. Some of them, including card sharks Jacques d'Amboise and Diana Adams, came over late in the evenings to play poker. The card playing could last all night. I would go off to sleep telling my guests, "Do what you want, I am going to bed." In the morning

I'd wake up to find them still there. They'd ask for breakfast and I'd tell them to take whatever they wanted from the refrigerator.

Australia remained a disaster to the end. The public was unreceptive. Not only didn't they care for our repertory, they even considered Jerry Robbins's *The Cage* to be pornographic. Everybody in the company had had enough and couldn't wait to leave. Shortly before we were to fly out of Melbourne, we got a message from the State Department, stating that they wanted us to perform in Okinawa for American servicemen. Betty was very much against this because, by now, the company was anxious to get to the last stop, Manila. But the State Department was insistent and because they were paying for the tour, Betty and I felt we should obey their instructions, no matter what.

Thanks to the State Department, a general made arrangements for aircraft to pick us up and fly us to Okinawa. What he had to offer was a military plane that had no seats, just benches along the sides, where the parachutists sit before they jump into the blue.

Betty was livid. "Absolutely not!" she said, "My dancers will not travel in that plane." Betty was always very protective of the company, but the State Department again insisted, and threatened not to pay for the return trip. Immediately, Betty and I got on the phone to Lincoln Kirstein in New York, who was equally furious.

"Fuck the State Department," he yelled. "If they don't want to pay, then I will pay."

So we relayed Lincoln's message to the State Department, which eventually agreed to pay for our trip home without the visit to Okinawa.

On our way directly to Manila, Betty spoke to me about our time in Australia. "Paul," she said jokingly, "This is the only thing we'll never be able to forgive you for."

In Manila, it was so hot that again nobody could stand being there. I don't think Betty Cage ever came out of her hotel room. It was so stifling that toe shoes melted in the heat. We all tried to cope with the situation, but Melissa Hayden kept raving that her shoes had melted. We ordered more, but they never arrived from New York. She was going on and on about her toe shoes until finally I couldn't take it anymore. "Give me those toe shoes," I demanded, and grabbed them from her. I brought them to an area that had a kitchen, lit the stove, and threw the shoes in the oven. Melissa was shocked. When I removed them, they were dried out and better than before. Melissa put on her newly-baked shoes, and gave the performance of a lifetime.

At that time there were still a lot of American soldiers and sailors in the Philippines, and they made being in Manila more tolerable. One evening, I met a sailor and invited him for a drink at the hotel where I was staying. He agreed, but said that he would have to stay over because it would be too late to return to the base. That was hardly a problem from my point of view. The following morning I got up at six to find he was already gone. I was sure that I had been robbed, and immediately looked for my passport and wallet. I found everything in order and on the small table near my bed a note that said "Thank you," plus two dollars.

George Balanchine : "Mr. B"

I would often meet George Balanchine in Europe, and once, after he was rehearsing the New York City Ballet at the Théâtre des Champs-Élysées in Paris, he invited me out to supper, at the Bar du Théâtre, opposite. A lot of the artists gathered there for drinks after a performance. We stood at the bar before our table was ready. Mr. B was in a very good mood that night and I thought I would take the opportunity to ask him a few things about himself and his work. I was always interested in how he choreographed, and when I asked him about composition, he told me that sometimes he preferred to choreograph directly from the score. I was amazed. I never knew anyone who choreographed in this way. Often, he said, he came into the studio with the ballet already worked out in his head. Considering Balanchine's musicality, I thought this was the perfect answer.

As the conversation continued, we started to talk about individual dancers, and men who were gay. He put down his drink and said, "You know, I don't care what people are doing in their private lives and whom they are sleeping with, boys or girls. However, there is one thing I don't like: when it shows on stage." And then he made a fist with his right hand, and punched it into his left palm a couple of times. It was his way of referring to sex. I found it comical to see the master choreographer of our time sending a message so primitively. "I don't care who they are," he continued, "I don't care if they are gay . . ." He then looked up at me with a funny grin on his face and said, "Aren't you gay?" and laughed.

"Why do you think so?" I asked.

"I know. I know," he said, beginning to wrinkle his nose, and make the little nervous, snorting sounds for which he was well known. But I wasn't about to let him off the hook. I decided to take my revenge.

"And what about you, Mr. B?" I asked.

"Never. Never," he said.

"Well," I said, "I am not so sure. I heard little stories . . ."

"What little stories?"

"About you and Diaghilev when you were choreographing for the *Ballets Russes*."

"Never. It never interested me," he said, while finishing his drink and rising from his chair. "Never," he repeated once again, and I knew it was time to drop the subject . . . for now.

Then we went to have dinner and continued to talk about dancers and Balanchine's ballets.

I remember another time when Balanchine invited me to come to the Paris Opera to attend a rehearsal. I was in Geneva, where my wife Ariane and I had a villa. At that time, Balanchine was artistic advisor at Geneva's Grand Theatre. Patricia Neary, one of the true stars of New York City Ballet, was the director of the ballet there, so Mr. B would come to the city often. Pat is an amazing director with a memory like a computer. She remembers all of Balanchine's ballets, and sets them in companies all over the world. She is one of the top coaches for *Apollo*. Mr. B liked her very much, and she ran the whole show in Geneva. I've always adored her, as a dancer and as a friend.

At one point, I had engaged two stars of the Bolshoi Ballet, Vladimir Vasiliev and Ekaterina Maximova, to dance the leads in *Giselle* at a dance festival in Nervi, Italy. But I had one problem: I needed to find a ballerina who could dance the Queen of the Wilis, a very demanding and important role that requires a strong technician with a great jump. I was having a difficult time finding just the right dancer until I thought of Patricia Neary, who was known for her technique, agility, and her jumps. I immediately informed Patricia she was going to dance Queen of the Wilis. She looked at me and said, "Paul, are you out of your mind? I never danced *Giselle* in my life, and I'm afraid to do it. It's out of the question."

"The role was made for you," I told her, and after some arm-twisting, she finally agreed. She danced the Queen of the Wilis and gave an amazing performance that brought down the house.

When Mr. B was in Geneva, he and Patricia Neary would come to our house for dinner, or we'd all go out to a restaurant near the theater. Balanchine loved Hungarian goulash, and if he was coming over, he'd call and request goulash, one of the things I know how to cook. Balanchine, a wine connoisseur, would also ask for a good Hungarian wine. I would run all over Geneva looking for a good Hungarian wine, which is not such an easy thing to find. Not in Switzerland, anyway. One time, the search paid off and I found a few bottles of Bull's Blood.

At dinner, I opened the wine, poured a bit for Balanchine, and then asked him what he thought of it. He raised his glass, brought it to his face, then took a bit in his mouth. We all stared at him, waiting for the verdict.

"This is good, good, good," he said, "If you've never drunk anything better."

Another evening, the mayor of Geneva hosted a dinner in honor of Balanchine and Pat Neary. Ariane and I were among the dozen or so guests. During the conversation, someone turned to Mr. B and said, "I heard that you are invited to be a judge at Varna," the most important ballet competition in Bulgaria.

Balanchine looked a little perplexed. "Varna? What is Varna? Why do they want me to go there and be a judge? Who will be there?"

I named Walter Terry from the *Herald Tribune* and other prominent critics and dancers.

"Oh my God," Mr. B said, "All those homosexuals. I don't want to go there. I'll send Jerry."

One time when I was booking City Ballet in the States, one local promoter in St. Louis had spent a lot of money getting the company and was desperate to have Maria Tallchief in *The Firebird*. That was her signature ballet. Unfortunately, that wasn't in the season's repertory, but he begged me to see if there was any way possible to add it to the program. I spoke to Betty when I came back to New York, and she told me to talk to Mr. B.

"Mr. B, we have a very good client, who has spent a lot of money and would love to have *Firebird*," I said.

"*Firebird*. It's an awful ballet. I hate it. What do they want *Firebird* for?"

"They want to see Maria."

"Maria? Maria? Maria?" Balanchine said, while starting to twitch and sniffle. "Well, if that's who they want, then give it to them!"

When Mikhail Baryshnikov found out that Balanchine was in Geneva, he came over from London, because he wanted to be coached in *Apollo* in preparation for performances at the Vienna Opera. In those days, Mr. B and Misha were not well acquainted, though they became very close later on. In fact, after Misha joined New York City Ballet, the two were like father and son.

I was at the rehearsal. Mr. B and I were sitting in the studio when he got up to talk to Baryshnikov. They began to speak in Russian and the next thing I knew, Mr. B came back to his seat and said, "Let's go. I want to have dinner." There was no rehearsal for him. I think he left Misha's coaching to Pat Neary. In my conversations with Mr. B I always had the feeling that he was against the star system.

Later on, he had to go to the Paris Opera when they were rehearsing some of his ballets, including *The Four Temperaments*. Because I was on my way to Paris also, Mr. B said, "If you want to come and see rehearsals, come."

"Thank you. I will," I told him.

We were sitting next to each other in the audience, watching the rehearsal: me, Mr. B, Boris Kochno, and Jerry Robbins. It began with the grand *pas de deux* from *La Bayadère*. Rudolf Nureyev was dancing with Noëlla Pontois, the prima ballerina of the Paris Opera. But when I turned to my side, Balanchine looked bored. A few minutes into the rehearsal, he asked me, "Who is that man on stage?" I didn't know if he was joking or not.

"That is Nureyev," I said.

"Ah," he said, twitching his nose.

Later, during the *pas de deux*, he again turned to me and said, "That man never saw *Bayadère*. He has absolutely no idea about the music. The tempi are all wrong and therefore I am not interested to stay. Let's go."

"But Mr. B, aren't you interested to stay for your ballets?"

"No, I am not, " he said. "Come. We go."

On the way out, Brigit Thom, one of the rehearsal directors, came over to talk to Mr. B. Since she could not speak English or French, only German, she asked if I would translate. She wanted to asked Balanchine if she could change one step in the ballet for Nureyev because he was having difficulty.

Balanchine looked at her and said, "You can change the whole ballet. I don't give a damn." Then he said to me, "Let's go out and have dinner," and off we went to the Grand Hotel.

Gala in Chicago

I was arranging a gala in Chicago with Balanchine's *Apollo* on the program. Helping me to put the gala together was Mrs. Geraldine Freund, who asked me to get Misha, by that time a major star. I went to his apartment on Park Avenue to ask if he would appear in the gala, but he seemed not very interested.

"Well, uh . . . I don't know . . . Why should I?" he said.

"Misha, you have to help me out. I need a big star."

He thought about it again and said, "If I can dance *Apollo*, I will come."

"Misha, that's not a problem." I knew he had already danced *Apollo* in Vienna, and all I'd have to do was ask Mr. B for his permission. Why should he refuse?

After I signed the contract with Baryshnikov, I went to the City Ballet offices to get Balanchine's permission. We greeted each other warmly and he asked me into his office.

"I'm making a gala . . ." I began.

"Ah," he said, wrinkling his nose, and making that little snort. "Gala . . . gala . . . Where?"

"Chicago," I answered.

"Ah, Chicago," he said.

"I'm here because I want to get your permission. I want to present *Apollo*."

"*Apollo*? With whom?" he asked.

"Baryshnikov," I said.

"Baryshnikov? No, no, no. Absolutely not!" He shouted at me. "I will not give you the permission. You cannot do it. I hate *Apollo*, I do not want to do *Apollo*, and he is not going to dance it."

"But Mr. B," I said, "you just gave him permission to do it in Vienna."

"I don't care what he does in Vienna. Here in America he is not going to do it." He was so hysterical I was afraid he was going to have a heart attack.

"Please, Mr. B. Calm down. Forget about it."

"Why can't I hate *Apollo*?" he yelled, "Stravinsky hated *Firebird*!"

I was very annoyed and didn't know what I was going to tell Misha. How could I tell him what Mr. B said?

111

The next morning I had to face the embarrassment and tell Misha the news. I first telephoned him to say I needed to talk to him immediately and then took a cab to his apartment. The minute he opened his door he said, "I know what you're going to tell me. He won't let me do it." Somehow, he knew.

"Listen to me, Misha. Meanwhile, another idea came to me. You should dance *The Prodigal Son*," another of Balanchine's ballets.

"I like the idea, Paul, but how are you going to get permission?" Misha asked.

"Don't worry. Leave that to me," I said.

"OK. If I can do *Prodigal Son*, I will come to Chicago."

The Ruth Page Company had *Prodigal Son* in its repertory. I flew to Paris, and went right to the Opera to see Ghislaine Thesmar, the prima ballerina whom Balanchine liked and often invited to dance with New York City Ballet. When I found her, I asked her if she wanted to dance with Baryshnikov, and she almost fainted. Misha was in his prime and the most celebrated dancer in the world.

"You are going to dance the siren in *Prodigal Son* with Misha in Chicago."

"But I never danced it in my life."

"Well, my dear, it's time you learned it," I said.

The Paris Opera Ballet was going to Russia for a tour. Ghislaine asked them to put *Prodigal Son* in the repertory so she'd have a chance to learn it, and they did.

Later on, she came to New York to rehearse with Misha, but insisted first on telling Balanchine what she was planning. They were very good friends and she felt that this was the right thing to do. At the City Ballet offices they greeted each other very warmly.

"What are you doing here?" Mr. B asked her.

"Paul is putting on a gala . . ."

"A gala . . . good . . . good . . ." he said, wrinkling his nose. "And what will you be dancing?"

"*The Prodigal Son*," she answered.

"With whom?" Mr. B asked.

"Misha," she said.

Silence. Mr. B said nothing, but I could see from his expression that he wasn't too happy about this. However, he agreed.

It was at this time that Nureyev was on Broadway dancing in *Nureyev and Friends*, which included *Apollo* in its program. I couldn't believe it! When I saw Balanchine I asked him about this. "You told me that you didn't want *Apollo* danced anymore, anywhere, by any of the stars. And now you give it to Nureyev?"

"Ah!! That's different. I am getting a lot of money for it and I need the money for the school. Hurok is paying me a lot of money for the rights. And I am not going to go stage it anyhow. I am going to send John Taras to put it on."

Lincoln Kirstein

Lincoln was a great man, very well-educated, with enormous knowledge of theater, ballet, and the arts. In many ways, he was larger than life, and he was respected throughout the world of culture, which experienced a great loss when he died a few years ago. I was very fond of Lincoln, and I think he liked me, but with Lincoln it was sometimes difficult to tell. There were days when I passed him by and said hello, and he'd just keep on walking. But when we did connect, and talked about ballet, he was always very sarcastic in his comments, and so was I. We were a perfect match, and, after a time, we developed a trust that enabled us to talk about other things besides dance and work.

When Lincoln and I discussed our private lives, he liked to talk about whom he was seeing, whom he was sleeping with, and who was next. One day, over lunch, he told me that he was very much in love with a young foreign student who was studying in New York. Lincoln wanted to invite him for a trip to Japan, and insisted that I accompany them. Lincoln was the type of a person you could never say no to. "Paul, I want to go to Japan with this fellow, and I want you to come along, too."

"Lincoln, what do you mean? I have my own business, I have . . . ," I tried to explain.

"Paul, I don't care what you have, you are coming with me. I will give you the dates."

I didn't dare say no, so I went to Japan.

We all stayed at the Imperial Hotel, naturally. He constantly told me that the connection he had with this young man was completely platonic. Because Lincoln was drinking and taking prescription pills for manic-depression, there were certain days when he was completely out of it. He'd walk around in a fog and become irrational. One day he ran out of his room and banged on my door with the wildest accusation. "I'm sure you've been having an affair with my boyfriend," he yelled.

"Lincoln," I said, "are you out of your mind?"

That same day he was invited to the residence of the American ambassador, but he was so drunk or high that I asked if I could accompany him. I didn't dare tell him my reasons, but in any case he wouldn't hear of my coming along.

I sat with his friend in the hotel, expecting Lincoln to be brought back in an ambulance. A few hours later, he returned completely sober, as if nothing had happened.

Actually, you never knew where you'd run into Lincoln. There used to be a famous Turkish bath, many years ago, in Harlem, on 125th Street, which was extremely gay. Believe it or not, it was one of the meeting places of high society. You'd be surprised whom you would run into. It was so popular that on the weekend, you'd have to wait on line for an hour or so before you could get in.

One day I arrived and ran into Lincoln Kirstein, a huge man wearing nothing but a small white towel. We were talking when suddenly a dancer from the New York City Ballet practically walked into us. He almost collapsed in embarrassment. He turned to me and said, "I had absolutely no idea what kind of a club this was . . ."

"Yes, darling," I said, "You thought it was a movie house. You made a mistake. We understand. We thought the same thing."

PART IV

GALA ATTRACTIONS

West Side Story

BECAUSE I WAS THE MOST PROMINENT IMPRESARIO in the Orient, I knew almost all of the important people in that theater world. One day, the owner of the Nissei Theater came to me with an idea. "Mr. Szilard," he said, "You are producing so many ballets and shows, why don't you bring a musical to Japan? We've never had one here before in the English language."

"That's a marvelous idea," I said, "What do you have in mind?"

"*West Side Story* from Broadway," he said.

Of course, the Leonard Bernstein–Stephen Sondheim–Jerome Robbins–Arthur Laurents collaboration is a landmark among American musicals. It still reverberates. The Broadway show was a huge hit, as was the movie version. It would be a coup for anyone to bring a production of *West Side Story* to Japan. However, I knew a lot of hurdles would have to be overcome. The Japanese wanted a very elaborate production, including stars from the original movie. I told them that it would be a very expensive show to produce, but I would investigate the possibilities.

I first had to decide whether the undertaking was financially feasible. While still in Japan, I had my secretary find out how many people there saw the movie version of *West Side Story*. The answer: about two million. We made a calculation and determined that if only one percent of the people who saw the movie turned out for the show, we'd have a minimum audience of twenty thousand people. With a number like that it seemed we'd be able to take the risk.

When I returned to New York, I immediately started contacting key people in the theater world. Jerry Robbins was very interested in the project, and we started our negotiations. Our cast consisted of people from the movie and from the Broadway and London stage productions: Don McKay (Tony) was a star of the London production, as were Marlys Walters (Maria) and Patti Karr (Anita). I hired Tucker Smith, who had played "Ice" in the movie. Jerry wanted Tony Mordente, who was "Action" in both the Broadway production and the movie, to be the dance director of the show.

After U.S. negotiations proceeded without a hitch, I signed the contract with the Nissei Theater. All the scenery was to be made in Japan, while the costumes were done by Albert Wolsky in the States. I arranged for about three or four weeks of rehearsal. It was much cheaper to take the whole company to Japan and rehearse there. Leonard Bernstein thought that certain musicians should be brought over from the States, primarily those who played five different instruments.

We also brought to Tokyo an American conductor, who was very short. The very elegant Nissei Theater had opened just before we started our rehearsals. It had a big ascending and descending orchestra pit. The conductor could not see the dancers and he asked if I could bring the orchestra up just a little bit. I agreed and conferred with the appropriate people in the theater. "Please bring up the pit," I said.

"Absolutely not. Impossible," they said.

"Why is it impossible?"

"We have the leading orchestras here, and we never had to raise the pit."

"I don't care who you've played here. Our conductor cannot see the dancers. If you don't bring it up, we can't perform."

Finally, they agreed to bring it up.

Opening night was a huge success, with the orchestra pit just where the conductor needed it to be. Each successive evening, however, the pit was lowered slightly, so that by the end of the first week, it was back in the basement.

Each weekend I'd scream and cause a scandal, and each Monday the pit would be raised. But by the end of the week, they always managed to bring it down.

In Tokyo alone we did over eighty performances. I think it was the first time a Broadway show in English was performed there. Theater ticket prices were very low at the time, and I charged three times the usual amount because it was so expensive to bring the show over, and did very little advertising. Nevertheless, in two or three days we sold out the entire Tokyo run. The show was so successful that we were asked to go on to Osaka, but after eighty-seven performances, most of the performers had had it and just wanted to return home.

Jerry wasn't very keen to come to Japan in the first place, but he told me that if I invited him to see the islands as well, he might join us. I agreed to pay for his vacation, ten days traveling around the Japanese islands with an interpreter. So Jerry came to Japan, and while he was there he shopped. He wanted tatami mats for his house, and pearls if he could get them at a good price. To be nice to me, he bought me a little netsuke. I had spent a fortune on him, and he dished out no more than a hundred bucks for me.

Upon our arrival we were greeted by dozens of journalists and a welcoming party of girls in kimonos. Jerry was very annoyed because he hated all this ceremony, particularly the constant bowing.

Tony Mordente had arrived earlier to begin the rehearsals, and everyone was waiting in terror of Jerry because of his reputation for being so tough to work with. I admired him for his precision and exactness and, indeed, I am the same way. Sometimes he would still be rehearsing at two in the morning because he wanted to make some changes and time was short.

One day he came to me and complained, "I don't like the jackets of the Sharks. They look terrible."

I turned to Wolsky and said, "Change the costumes."

Everybody was shocked to hear me say that because they knew it would cost a small fortune to make such a change at the last minute. But I wanted to please Jerry. Even he looked surprised that I didn't argue with him.

The next problem was the ballet shoes. The dancing was so

difficult that after a few days of rehearsal many of the dancers' shoes had holes in them. Every minute we had to wait while dancers changed their shoes, and soon we were running out of shoes. I went around looking for Jerry and asked him, "What do I do, the shoes are falling to pieces? We can't afford to replace them all the time."

To my surprise, he wanted to be accommodating to me and said, "Do it in sneakers." And that became the first time the dancers danced in sneakers in the show.

Toward the end of our stay in Japan, Jerry approached me and said, "Paul, do me a favor. Instead of flying back to New York, I'd like to have a ticket to travel around the world."

"All right," I agreed, "I will arrange it." Of course, it was very expensive, but I wanted to make Jerry happy and the show was a huge success. The public went wild for *West Side Story*. People were fighting to see the show. It seemed as if all of Japan had come to the theater. After we closed and left Tokyo, several local productions of *West Side Story* popped up, but they were just poor imitations of the real thing. And they were performed in Japanese.

Dancers of Bali

I've always been fascinated by Indonesia. I had traveled to Jakarta several times, and each time I grew more impressed with the people and the culture. It always seemed to me a country of artists, especially dancers. It became a dream of mine to see Bali and their famed dancers, and I was told by a few people that the best Balinese dancing was in the village of Tabanan. It was not performed by a professional troupe but by the village dancers. A local promoter, who spoke English, took me there, where we were introduced to Mario of Tabanan, the head of the local dance group. Mario was considered the Nijinsky of Balinese dancing. In the 1920s, he had created a new form of Balinese dancing, Kebyar, which was performed in a seated position before a trompong, an instrument in the gamelan orchestra consisting of a row of gongs in a frame. Mario was in his seventies when I met him, quite a charming man, with a wonderfully expressive face and body. Every expression, from humor to dignity to sadness, seemed to be etched in the lines in his face. When he reached his hand out to greet me, I felt that I was immediately in the presence of a unique soul. He seemed to dance standing still.

A few days later I was able to see the Tabanan dancers for myself. It was a very hot and sunny day. The local promoter and I made our way from my hotel, and minutes later, walked through woods and found ourselves in front of a Balinese temple. All Balinese dancing that I'm familiar with is done in front of an ancient temple, in the evening. The Balinese dance to a gamelan. The rhythms and the melodies of their music get handed down from generation to generation. The instruments are painted and look like works of art. The Tabanan Palace Gamelan, locally known as the "Gong Pangkung," is the most ancient and famous in Bali.

At night, very late, they danced to the flickering light of kerosene lamps. The girls who dance are very young, about twelve or fourteen years old, while the boys are much more mature. While I watched them I felt transported to another world. Their dance dramas are filled with colorful characters including monsters, monkeys, and kings. The dancers have an incredible stage presence—even though they then had no idea what a stage was in the Western sense.

As soon as I saw them that first time I knew I wanted to bring them to the United States. I flew back home, went to Columbia Artists Management, and met with the Chairman of the Board, Mr. Schang. As far as I was concerned, there were really only two important impresarios at the time, Schang and Hurok. And I always preferred Schang. I found Hurok uneducated, but Schang, a newspaper man, was an art collector and understood theater, dance, and painting. He and I had a few long talks about the Dancers of Bali, and finally after our third or fourth meeting, he said, "Paul, I believe in you. I like the way you approach such a project. I trust you, and will back you up." So Columbia and Mr. Schang supported me in my efforts to bring the dancers to the States.

Once we agreed, I returned to Bali to organize the show. The Dancers of Bali had never danced on a Western stage before, and I felt I had to come up with a program that would be accepted here. Many of their dances were very slow and repetitive; I wanted something that would work for an American audience, and from my experience, I knew the public would not stand for anything too long and too slow-paced. I went to Bali with the goal of setting some of their dances, though I did not know if that was possible.

I stayed in Bali for three weeks and worked with Mario on the program. It was a pleasure to work with him because of the respect we felt for one another. He knew that I had been a dancer, and held me in the highest regard. Through a translator I explained that we must shorten some of the dances for the public in the Western world. Mostly, we made cuts in repetitions. Even when there was no interpreter around, we were somehow able to understand what the other person was feeling.

"I would like to cut it without disturbing the artistic integrity and meaning of the dance," I said to Mario through an interpreter. "Where do you think it can be cut?" Though Mario and most of the village elders had never been away from Tabanan, they trusted me, and agreed to cut some of the pieces, without disturbing the artistry of the choreography.

Mario was already in his 70s, as mentioned, and was long retired from dancing. All the same, I told him, "I must have you on stage." And after a while, he agreed. He mentioned another male dancer, Gusti Raka, who was much younger and, a fabulous technician, was the only one who still danced Kebyar. Raka's footwork was incredible. In his own way, he was a bravura dancer. Even though Raka came from another province and never danced with Mario's group, he agreed to come to America and dance with them.

At that point, I knew I was going to have a sensational attraction. I flew back to the States, met with lighting designer Tom Skelton, and brought him back with me to Bali. I wanted him to see the presentation there—the temple, parasols and palm trees that are part of the dance—and I wanted him to recreate that atmosphere for the States. It wouldn't do for Tommy to learn about the dance through books and films. He needed to be there with me to pick up the atmosphere and the feeling firsthand.

I decided to take the dancers to Europe first, and chose Lausanne, Switzerland for their premiere in 1957. It was at a spanking new theater, and one day the manager was running around calling for me: "Mr. Szilard, Mr. Szilard, please, you must do something. The dancers are peeing on the floor instead of the toilets." They did their business in a corner of the theater because at home, they had no toilets, and they now were simply following their familiar ways.

Back in New York, when I wanted to hire Tommy Skelton I learned he was still an apprentice and not yet in the union, and therefore ineligible to work on Broadway. The man who took his place as lighting designer did a terrible job. I always respect other people's work unless I find that it's jeopardizing the production. Each time I attended the rehearsals I said, "Don't you think it's a little bit dark?" And he would always say, "No, no. It will be all right." But it seemed to get darker and darker, until the dancers could hardly be seen. A few days before the opening, I said, "Listen, this stage is too dark. You have to make it lighter." Furiously, he turned on me and said, "Look, I am director of lighting, I like it, and this is the way it is going to be."

"Well, I am the producer, and I hate the lighting, and if you don't change it, you're out," I answered.

Since he refused to make any changes, I threw him out of the theater. He ran screaming to the union, and as a result I was fined. But I was then able to go back to Tommy and say, "You take it over." The job of lighting director was now his. That was the first time he lit a show on Broadway, and he went on to become one of the most important lighting designers of the time.

In addition to the lighting, there were other technical glitches. In New York's ANTA Theater we had terrible problems because the Balinese instruments are considered religious items, and the musicians and dancers would not allow the stagehands, or any-body, to touch them. The stagehands protested. We had to have meetings to explain to the union the religious nature of the instruments that allowed them to be carried or touched only by the dancers. After a few sessions, the union gave the dancers a special dispensation to carry their own instruments. Before each performance the dancers and the musicians prayed.

I only prayed before the premiere.

Finally, it was time for opening night. The theater was packed, and you could feel the excitement in the air as the lights dimmed and the audience became hushed. As the curtain was raised, the theater was quiet, and Mario was sitting on the floor in a traditional pose. In a few seconds there was the sound of sky-shattering thunder from the gamelan instruments as Mario rose to dance. Everyone felt that they had been transported to Bali. The theater reverberated as the audience erupted in applause.

The performance was a tremendous success. The reviews were fabulous. And we soon had people sleeping on the street trying to get tickets.

The Dancers of Bali were such a hit that Ed Sullivan came to see them a few times and decided he wanted them on his famous television show. Since we were going on tour, I felt we could use the publicity. I accepted Ed Sullivan's invitation . . . to what turned out to be a nightmare.

"I don't like the decor," Ed said, "we will use our own."

He offered a velour backdrop, filled with sequins, in the shape of a church. It was awful.

Ed Sullivan showed great interest in Raka and particularly a moment in his dance when he did a difficult backward kick and kicked the train of his costume. Sullivan, standing with his arms familiarly folded as he watched a rehearsal, turned to me and said, "Paul, cut the costume. I want to see his feet." The comment was not the product of any artistic sense but of Sullivan's commercial taste.

"It is not possible. His costume is part of the dance," I said.

"I don't care. I want to see his foot. I want it cut."

"Ed, we cannot do that."

"But I insist," he said.

Since we needed the publicity, I agreed to compromise and hemmed the costume a bit. Poor Raka couldn't believe it.

When the dancers had finished, Ed Sullivan took one of the smallest girls in his arms and stood with her in front of the curtain. "Who am I?" he asked her, staring right into the television camera. She had been prepped backstage. Over and over, he would ask the question, and she would reply.

"Ed Sul-li-van." It had been banged into her head until she got it right.

"Do you like me?" he asked.

"Yes."

He kissed her. Then he put her down with careless indifference and a stagehand walked her off.

I brought the Dancers of Bali back for two more tours. Before they returned to the States for the first of these, I got a call from the director of the Arie Crown Theater, part of the McCormick Center in Chicago. "I want to get the Dancers of Bali," he said, but he had one special demand: that we open the show in Chicago. I told him we couldn't do that because I needed the New York press and publicity for touring. But he was insistent. "I was told by [the critic] Claudia Cassidy that I must have the dancers and that they are fantastic. I want them for three weeks."

"Well, they are very expensive," I said.

"I don't care. If she says it's good, then I will take it."

"OK. If that's the case, then we will open in Chicago."

We arrived in Chicago on what must have been their coldest day on record. The snow was up to our necks, and the company arrived in traditional, lightweight sarongs, with no shoes on their feet. The Marshall Fields department store had agreed to dress the dancers at the airport just for the publicity value. When the plane landed on the snowy tarmac, the Balinese dancers and musicians were met by people who covered them with blankets, then hurried them into the terminal. Inside, there was a display of shoes on one side, and clothes on the other. Unfortunately, there was no one to measure the dancers and soon they were putting on coats with sleeves that hung to the floor, or forcing their feet into shoes that were clearly the wrong fit. But the dancers all had a good time and the children were ecstatic.

We had tried to find a decent hotel for the company that was near the theater but because the choices were so dismal we finally had to settle for a run-down place that had once been the headquarters of Al Capone. A photographer from *Life* magazine came by one day to take pictures of the Balinese dancers in Al Capone's bathtub.

In the hotel there was a Jewish delicatessen. When I explained to the owner about the dancers and their diet, he said, "We can make you whatever you'd like. If you want Indonesian, we can do that. Just tell us what you want." We took one of the dancers to the kitchen to demonstrate how to prepare their special rice. As a result, the entire cast and crew could be seen sitting in the kosher deli having pure Balinese food. Everybody loved those Indonesian children in the kosher deli.

Mahalia Jackson

Mahalia Jackson was an incredible woman, as exciting an artist as Judi Jamison. When I decided I wanted to arrange a concert for her in Hawaii, I went to her agent at William Morris and we worked out an agreement. Mahalia was afraid of flying, so she and her entourage of at least seven went by ship. She traveled first class, and was paid to perform on board. And since sneaky Mahalia didn't tell me about that concert, she could keep all the proceeds. In Hawaii, she performed at night in an open-air theater.

Unfortunately, we didn't have the best weather for an outdoor concert. It rained continuously and everything was nearly washed out. She had seven thousand people in her audience, instead of the ten thousand expected, and that wasn't enough to cover expenses, so I lost money.

The next morning, the sun came out, and I told Mahalia to go sit in the sun because she was getting a cold.

"What the hell do I need a suntan for? I've already got one," she said.

"Mahalia, I want to invite you for dinner," I told her.

"My God," she said, "you lost money on me and now you want to take me to dinner."

She was so heavy that she had difficulty walking. Whenever she put on a proper shoe to go on stage, she was in a lot of pain. When she came into the wings, she ripped the shoes off.

Mahalia was very religious and had her own church in Chicago. And of course she sang gospel on stage, but you should have heard her language when this devout Christian got off. She cursed like a truck driver. "For Christ sake, you play like shit," she was fond of telling the musicians when they finished a performance.

Later on, I made a contract for her to perform in Japan, but she died while we were still making arrangements.

Kovach and Rabovsky, Szilard, and Massine

Nora Kovach and her husband and partner, Istvan Rabovsky, were prima ballerina and premier danseur of the Budapest State Opera Ballet. His technique was sharp and impeccable—even today, it's difficult to find anybody of his caliber. Artistically, he wasn't particularly expressive, but he was an exciting technician. Nora, however, was flawless in every way—a ballerina in the Plisetskaya category. As partners, they brought the house down. In 1953, when they were guesting in East Berlin, they defected via subway to the Western zone. Because they disappeared during a performance, it was regarded as a huge scandal. When they crossed into West Berlin, someone from Sol Hurok's office was waiting for them. Clearly, this was a well-planned escape. Later that year, they made their American debut. And offstage they married, divorced, re-married, and redivorced. They even survived a sinking ship.

Once they were in the U.S., the Rabovskys were represented by impresario Sol Hurok. When he brought them to New York to perform—first on the *Ed Sullivan Show*—they were a sensation, not only for their dancing but also because they were the first dancers to defect from a communist country. This was before Nureyev, before Baryshnikov, and before Makarova. Soon, how-ever, they grew unhappy with Hurok, because he had them danc-ing in huge auditoriums and stadiums and in places like Las Vegas, where he could make a lot of money but where they were neither respected as artists nor treated as stars.

When I first saw them dance, I was sure I could make a suc-cessful tour with them. But first I had to win Hurok's approval, so one day we all got together at the Russian Tea Room in New York City and I explained my interest. Hurok agreed to let me have the Rabovskys for my 1955 tour of South America, arranged because I had been invited to become guest choreog-rapher at the Teatro Municipal in Rio de Janeiro. Hurok was pleased about all this, and let them out of their U.S. contract with him temporarily for the tour.

While we toasted the Rabovskys over lunch, Hurok raised his glass and said, "I have a wonderful idea for Nora and Istvan."

I could tell that this made them a bit nervous. I felt the same way.

"The Rabovskys should dance Vienna waltzes," Hurok said, and there was dead silence at the table for a couple of seconds. What an awful idea, I thought, but that was Hurok's taste.

The invitation to Rio was for an eight-week engagement, after which Léonide Massine would be guest choreographer for an ad-ditional two months. During my time, I was to put on some stan-dard ballets from the repertoire and choreograph two new ballets for the Rabovskys. They were one of the greatest dance attrac-tions in the world, and in Rio, their success proved overwhelming.

Nora was known for making scandals, whether it was in her

dressing room, on stage, or off. One day while we were rehearsing at the opera house, Nora behaved so badly that I threatened to throw her out of the theater and to replace her with her understudy. As naughty as she could be, she also had a sharp sense of humor. I was standing at the other end of the stage from her when she got on her knees and crawled towards me with her hands clasped, saying, "Please forgive me, forgive me, forgive me." I started laughing so hard it was difficult to remain mad at her.

On opening night for my ballet, Massine and I shared a box. The entire evening I waited for his opinion, but he did not say a word to me, good or bad. I was the newcomer, he was the established star, and I thought he should have been more generous.

However, one day, Massine came to me in Rio and said, "Paul, I hear you are a wonderful businessman. That you are very clever. Why don't we form a ballet company? You should get me some backers."

"But what would be my position in the company? What will I do?"

"The name will be Massine Ballet and we will find someplace for you." Probably the stage door man! All he wanted was for me to raise money for him.

Outside the United States, Hurok did not handle Kovach and Rabovsky. They guested with many companies around the world, including the London Festival Ballet, under the direction of Anton Dolin, and performed in the Liceo Opera House in Barcelona under my management. Wherever they danced, they sold out the house. Audiences were spellbound. They were technically so sensational that they could execute feats that were attempted only by the Russians in those days. Their lifts were incredible. While they were performing the *Don Quixote pas de deux* in Spain, the dancers around them became quite jealous. Backstage sometimes proves as compelling as the performance.

One afternoon, I arrived in the theater, and went to the rehearsal director and asked, "How is the house?"

"Ah," he said, "completely sold out."

That night I went to the theater, and as the lights dimmed, I looked around and saw only about half the seats occupied. I asked the management what had happened and was told, "Just wait."

Sure enough, when the time came for the Rabovsky's *pas de deux*, the house filled up. People came in just to see them, not caring about the rest of the company. And they were such a sensation, they must have had about twenty curtain calls.

That's when the company became jealous, and later began to play unspeakable tricks. In one subsequent performance, while the Rabovskys were dancing the coda, the middle of the *pas de deux*, the curtain suddenly came down. I was backstage at that moment and started screaming at the stagehands, "What are you doing? They are still dancing!" The stagehands told me it was an accident. But it was no accident. I was fuming and ordered them to raise the curtain at once. When the curtain opened, Nora and Istvan continued the coda as if nothing had happened, and the audience, thinking they were seeing an encore, became only more appreciative.

Nora and Istvan were aboard the Andrea Doria on their way back to the States during that summer of 1956 when the ship collided with the Stockholm off Nantucket and eventually sank. Other boats in the vicinity came to rescue the passengers as the ship was towed to shore. *Life* magazine was there in time to photograph the passengers as they climbed down from the ocean liner and were brought to safety. When Nora learned that reporters from *Life* were waiting there, cameras in hand, she rushed back to her soggy cabin. "I have to put on lipstick. I can't come down the stairs without having makeup on!"

Marcia Haydée

Some years ago, when the Stuttgart Ballet came to the Metropolitan Opera, I was invited to the performance and to the gala afterwards. At the party, a charming young woman kept walking by me, smiling, and saying hello. Finally, she stood in front of me and said, "You don't know who I am, do you?"

"Who are you?" I am always very blunt.

"I'm Marcia Haydée."

She was the Brazilian-born prima ballerina of the Stuttgart, and an amazing dancer.

She continued, "When you were guest ballet master at the Teatro Municipal, I was in the *corps de ballet*."

Making a joke, I said, "Darling, I don't know people in *corps de ballet*. I only know stars." We both laughed, and from then on we stayed friends.

Galas: Chicago, Munich, Moscow

In Chicago I produced many galas at the Opera House with Mrs. Geraldine Freund, whom I met through Jurgen Schneider, the former ballet master of American Ballet Theatre. She wanted to become involved in the dance world but did not know where to start, so Jurgen suggested that she contact me. I don't think she even knew how to spell the word "ballet" when we met. She had a flair for the arts, but was difficult to work with and capable of outbursts of bitchiness. Gradually, however, we found a way to work together, and became good friends. I just love her. Over the years, we signed all the prominent stars, and Chicago became famous for these galas. I made the contracts, and Mrs. Freund made out the checks. Unfortunately, she was difficult about money. When it came to paying the dancers, we'd end up screaming at each other. Once I threw a checkbook at her when she wasn't ready. She was never ready, and all the great artists had to line up for their money, as if they were on the dole, even though she insisted on having those big names.

At one of the Chicago galas Gelsey Kirkland and her partner Patrick Bissell danced the *Don Quixote pas de deux*. It was already known in the dance world that Gelsey was having problems in her personal life. Her habits had become very strange. She was completely incommunicado. She usually didn't show up at the theater until the very last minute, when the curtain was about to go up. Mrs. Freund, a doctor, and I stood in the wings that night waiting for disaster to strike. During one of the fouetté turns of the dance, Gelsey fell. The audience gasped. She got up and admonished the floor with her fan, as if the reason for the tumble was a hole in the stage and had nothing to do with her. People erupted in laughter because Gelsey was so funny about it. But it was terrible behavior for such a star.

I invited Jacques d'Amboise and Suzanne Farrell to dance at a gala I helped to organize at the Munich Opera House. Suzanne was no more than seventeen at the time, and I believe this was the first time she performed in Europe. She was beautiful, shy, and distant. She and Jacques danced *Thaïs*, choreographed by d'Amboise, and the *pas de deux* from Balanchine's *Episodes* to music by Webern. They were a huge success.

On another occasion, I remember talking to Mr. B about *Apollo*, possibly his most famous ballet. I asked him whom he considered to be the best in the role.

It didn't take very long for him to answer.

"Watch Jacques," he said, "and you will see . . ."

And I did.

And he was.

There was to be a major gala at the Bolshoi in Moscow to commemorate UNESCO's 40th anniversary, in 1986. I was approached by the Soviet government television organization, which was inviting dancers from all over the world, to bring dancers from the U.S. I decided upon Merrill Ashley from the New York City Ballet and Kevin McKenzie from American Ballet Theatre. They were to dance the *Tchaikovsky pas de deux* from Balanchine.

We arrived in Moscow and were assigned to the Russiyo Hotel, near the Kremlin. It was an large, ugly structure built during the Soviet regime. We got there to find that all the dancers who would be performing in the gala were standing around waiting for rooms. Most were beside themselves because they wanted a different room, a bigger bed, another view. Carla Fracci, the Italian ballet star, who arrived with an entourage, refused the room given her. She demanded a suite and sat in the lobby until she got one. Merrill, Kevin, and I weren't happy with our rooms either, but not being divas, no one made a big fuss about it. As a matter of fact, my bed was too hard, but I was happy because that's what I needed for my bad back. It turned out to be the best night's sleep of my life.

On each floor was an old babushka to whom you had to give your room key every time you left the hotel. She would bring tea to your room each morning, and I would give her a dollar, which was against the rules.

When we went to the Bolshoi for rehearsals, we found that they did not use linoleum on their floors but stretched canvas instead, which could be treacherous. Merrill and Kevin were hysterical at first because they had never performed on canvas before, but they danced beautifully, and became the stars of the gala.

The translator who was assigned to me was probably a KGB lady. She would not let me make a step without her. One day, I told her I was very tired and just wanted to rest in my room. After she left, I immediately went downstairs, rented a car, and on my own visited the sensational Pushkin museum. Next day, when she found out, she almost had a heart attack, telling me that I had put her in grave danger.

When I was leaving Moscow, she picked me up in an official government car to take me to the airport. I wanted to drop off some publicity photos with the cultural attaché of the U.S. embassy, because I hoped to bring other companies in the future. So, on our way, I asked her if I could stop at the embassy to deliver my envelope. She flat out refused without knowing what I was carrying. Finally, I said, "Well, if you want to see what's in it, open it up." She calmed down a bit when she saw the photographs. At the airport, I gave her all of my leftover rubles, and she was delighted.

Melissa Hayden

When I booked Melissa Hayden and Jacques d'Amboise into a gala on Long Island, during intermission, the local promoter came to me and said, "Mr. Szilard, the public is very annoyed because Miss Hayden is not in her best form."

"Well, that happens. She's probably tired," I said, and went backstage to speak to her.

"Melissa," I said, "You have to pull yourself together. The audience feels that you are not giving your all."

"WHAT?" she croaked in her unique, gravelly voice, "I'll show them." She took out a needle and stabbed herself in the hip with a dose of vitamin B. She then grabbed a box of kleenex, and an oxygen bottle, and took a few deep breaths. Her eyes seemed to get bigger by the second. "Now they are going to see something," she said, and stormed out as if she were going to battle. Needless to say, she was sensational.

The Role of the Critic

Why are critics necessary? Whom are they for? For me, the answer is simple: The role of the critic is to educate us. Though I have always believed that people should make up their own minds about a performance, critics do serve a purpose by offering the layman knowledge of the art form, whether it be ballet, painting, or classical music.

To my mind, some of the critics today are extremely well-educated and know more than most dancers. However, most critics are removed from what dancers do and feel onstage. There are many nuances and subtleties in dance that get lost in the space between the stage and the critic's notebook. In my opinion, the ideal critic would be a person who was a principal dancer, someone who would know what it's like to perform and, therefore, understand the emotion involved. Many times, I feel that the critics lack that sensibility. I'm sure that many of the well-known critics took class and studied dance, but that does not make them dancers. That experience merely gives them knowledge of the dance vocabulary, without which they couldn't do their job.

I cannot understand how two critics can watch the same choreography, and one will think it's the best ever created, and the other will pan it from start to finish. Certainly, there has to be an artistic line that defines the performance, there have to be indisputable constants, recognizable to all. Is it a work of art? That's a question that goes beyond liking and not liking. I am not talking about the execution of the choreography. Once the artistic merits of a work are established, then the critic can take off with his or her own opinion. But the facts should come first. Is there art in it or not?

When I was a dancer, I danced all over the world and received both favorable and unfavorable criticism. However, no matter what was said about me, I was always recognized as an artist. As a dancer, I was purely classical. When I did my own concerts, the *"recital de danse,"* in the manner of Harald Kreutzberg and others, the critic and the public judged me on my complete performance as a concert artist, because I was obliged to do my own choreography. On such occasions valid judgments could be made about an artist, because you not only had to be a dancer, you had to be a musician, and you had to have imagination.

We live in a different world today. What happened in my period doesn't exist anymore because people are thinking differently. They've been brought up differently. A lot has to do with education, and a lot has to do with where you were born. I was always interested in the arts, even before I knew I wanted to be a dancer. In school, the whole idea was to expose children to as much as possible. We were obliged, whether we liked them or not, really to learn the subjects we were taught. Why did I have to learn Latin? I did not want to become a priest or a doctor. Regardless, I had to study Latin for eight years. As a matter of fact, I failed once, and had to repeat a whole year. That whole summer Latin was beaten into my brain. Seventy years later, I still remember how to conjugate my verbs. In my time we could not choose what we wanted to learn. Today schools are too permissive in deciding which subjects students must learn. And sometimes kids think they have nothing to learn, and graduate with a diploma that has no meaning.

Eight years of Latin: do you think I *needed* it? I'm not the Pope. In looking back on my education, I feel that if I had allowed to study only what I wanted to learn, I would have missed out on a lot.

I am not a critic, but I am not afraid to offend people. I am known for that!

Anna Galina and Le Théâtre d'Art du Ballet

The Russian pianist, Kopeikine, who worked for George Balanchine and New York City Ballet, told me about a young dance company for which he also played. Le Théâtre d'Art du Ballet from Paris was new—in fact, barely getting off the ground, and he wanted to know if I'd be interested in booking them. At the time, their main focus was on Fokine, not just *Les Sylphides* but minor Fokine ballets as well.

Anna Galina, whose real name was Evelyn Cournand, was the prima ballerina of the company, which she had founded in 1957 with her teacher Tatiana Piankova. Anna was wealthy, half Hungarian, half French, and took her name from her two favorite ballerinas: Anna Pavlova and Galina Ulanova, with whom she would become great friends later on.

I decided to take on "Le Théâtre d'Art du Ballet" and then continued to represent them for twenty-six years, taking them around the world six times. It was a good company, but not a first-rate company. What it was, was a unique company.

Before I became involved with them, Anna and her company had debuted in Monte Carlo, and by all accounts, the premiere was a disaster. Anna, very young, had been following the advice of people who were interested only in her money. In those early days, one critic wrote that her mentor, Madame Piankova, was a fake and had never danced in the Pavlova company. Anna sued that critic and won. Offered a check as part of the settlement, Anna took it and tore it in two. "I don't need your money," she said, "but you must apologize." The newspaper had to admit in print that their critic had lied. After that, Anna refused to dance in France ever again.

Anna was so wealthy that people would take advantage of her. Many of the critics were against her because they considered her just a rich girl who thought she could dance. In truth, she was not a great dancer, but she was quite good, with a great stage personality that convinced me to book her company. Also, she had complete financial backing. Hurok, a good friend of Anna's father, had wanted to handle the company and was furious to learn that I got there first. He then tried everything to get the company away from me, but Anna Galina admired me, and would not work with him.

Most companies want to dance on consecutive nights because they need the money. Not so with this one. When I booked Le Théâtre d'Art du Ballet, Anna made it clear that there were to be no bookings on consecutive evenings. Ideally, they would perform no more than a couple of times a week. For me, this was perfectly fine. Her father, Édouard Cournand, held the American distribution rights to Lanvin, the French perfumery, but although he was extremely rich he was forever trying to think of ways of getting Anna to close the company, which was always in the red. After each tour ended, I would go to his office and present the bills to Mr. Cournand.

"Mr. Szilard, this company has already cost me over $300,000," he once said.

"Is that all?" I replied.

"Mr. Szilard, how much do I have to pay you to close your office?" he would ask me.

"Mr. Cournand, you wouldn't have that amount of money," I replied.

"Mr. Szilard, is there any chance that in my daughter's lifetime the company will even make one dollar?"

"Absolutely not. But why do you want to make money when

the great companies, like New York City Ballet, American Ballet Theatre, never see a penny? To have a ballet company is a luxury."

"Yes, I've heard that before," he said, paying the bills.

I told Anna that she had to add to her repertory a major ballet by a well-known choreographer. Since she liked Massine she asked him if he would do a new ballet for her. Much to everybody's surprise, because he was so famous and hers was such a small company, he accepted, and proceeded to create the ballet *Ballade*. She must have paid a fortune for it. Natalia Gontcharova, who had frequently collaborated with Serge Diaghilev for the Ballets Russes, was engaged to do the costumes. *Ballade*, with music by Fauré, was not very memorable. It was vaguely Greek, or anyway mythological, with dancers dressed in flesh-colored body tights to give the impression they were naked. I wished they were because the costumes were so awful.

Anna spent her money on the best directors, the best scenery, the best costumes. She paid her company throughout the year, whether they danced or not—a rarity in the dance world. My first tour with them was to Japan, where they were a success. After that we had several three- and four-month tours to all parts of the world. Once, in Nairobi, Kenya, we were to perform at a small theater that was completely sold out. But when we went backstage, it was so dirty Anna refused to unpack.

"My costumes have just been cleaned, and I am not going to take them out here. Cancel all the performances," she ordered.

"But it's sold out," I said.

"Then pay it back," she said, and that was final.

In India, we were to perform at a charity performance in Bombay. Our contract stated that the company would dance to piano accompaniment. When we arrived, I went to the president of the local philharmonic society and said, "Madam, we are about to begin rehearsing. Where is the piano?"

"Piano? Didn't you bring the piano?" she asked.

"Madam, for one performance, you expect us to bring a piano from Paris to Bombay?"

"But you have it in the contract, piano accompaniment."

"Madam, that refers to the concert pianist, not the piano," I said.

Finally, she agreed to let us use the piano she had in her salon.

Again the performance was sold out. We arrived with all our scenery only to find the stage was not equipped for it. With no place to hang the scenery, we had to perform without it. After the rehearsal, a member of the local charity who had helped to organize the performance came up to Anna and said, "But we expected scenery. The contract stated costumes and scenery."

Anna had a very good sense of humor. She looked at the woman and said, "You want to see scenery? Come with me," whereupon she led her from backstage to a garden where all the trunks were stacked. "That, my dear, is the scenery," Anna said, and walked away.

In Calcutta, when Anna was dancing *Les Sylphides*, one of her major ballets which she always danced very well, I was backstage when I heard her screaming. I rushed to the wings to see that there were rats darting back and forth across the stage. Anna became so frightened that she didn't want to go on, but finally she did.

Léonide Massine owned an island off the coast of Naples that was given to him by Diaghilev. (When Massine died, his children sold it to Nureyev.) One day Massine came to Anna with what he presented as a fabulous idea. She should develop his empty island for a summer dance festival to be known as "Massine's Festival." But Anna was very smart and after telling me what Massine had proposed, said to me, "I wonder what he has in store for me?"

So we went by boat to see the island and found absolutely nothing there. Everything would have had to be built from scratch. Anna turned to me and said, "If I buy this island I know what will happen. I will be in the *corps de ballet* and write checks."

Because Anna was a very close friend of Ulanova's, I could never understand why she didn't advise Anna to take on another teacher besides Piankova. Ulanova came to Anna's studio many times to watch class and must have seen for herself that Piankova was a good teacher, but not good enough to make a prima ballerina out of Anna. Piankova was well educated and had a very distinguished manner. I liked her more as a person than as an artist.

Mr. Cournand called Piankova "Rasputin" because she had such a fierce hold on his daughter. Certainly Piankova benefited from continuing the status quo. Anna showered her with gifts: cars, fur coats, etc. Anna had lost her mother when she was very young, and Piankova was like her guru, part mother, part sister, and part friend.

But Piankova had a weak heart. One day in Paris, while riding with Anna in a taxicab on the way to a hospital to get her heart checked, she had a heart attack. She died right in the taxicab.

When Piankova died, Anna went off the deep end. She disbanded the company. She wouldn't give away any of Madame's personal belongings. She hired trucks to carry away the scenery and the costumes, as well as everything that belonged to Piankova, including furs and couture clothing, and had everything burned outside of Paris. After Piankova's death, I heard that Anna kept the body in her apartment for a couple of days, placing ice around it in a bed, while she herself slept on the floor nearby. After a few days, she allowed the body to be cremated. Anna had Piankova's ashes sewn into a garment that she wore for a while.

Though the company was dissolved, every once in a while Anna came to New York, where she kept an apartment in the Plaza Hotel, and we'd get together. She established a foundation in the name of Madame Piankova for the children of India. Her lawyer in New York was an old friend of the family. She trusted him completely and regarded him as the greatest. He set up the foundation, handled Anna's money, and never sent her a bill. I always told her to be very careful. I had never heard of a lawyer being so altruistic.

When Anna returned to Paris, she was very unhappy, with no more Madame Piankova and no more dance company. Though she was then only in her 40s, she lost interest in life.

One morning, I opened the *New York Times* and saw an article that said Anna's lawyer was being sued for stealing money from a client. After reading this, I cut it out of the paper and immediately called her in Paris.

Her maid answered the phone and I said, "I must talk to Mademoiselle at once. This is Paul Szilard."

The maid could hardly talk because she was crying. She told me, slowly, that Anna had committed suicide the day before.

While she was still dancing, Anna had contracted cancer of the breast, but had refused to have an operation. I suspect that the cancer had developed so far that this was one of the reasons, among others, that she committed suicide.

Lucia Chase and American Ballet Theatre

I had been asked by presenters in Europe to bring over a company with a true classical background, and the only large company that seemed suited was American Ballet Theatre, under the direction of Lucia Chase. Chase herself was trained as a classical dancer, and had worked with such luminaries as Mikhail Mordkin and Michel Fokine. At that time, I really admired ABT. They had wonderful training, excellent dancers and choreography, and a very good *corps de ballet.* This would be a ballet company that could well represent the United States. I approached Lucia Chase about taking ABT to Japan and to Europe. She was very interested and agreed after discussing the idea with her board.

There were true stars in the company back then and they lit up the world. Today, we don't have stars with such personalities. Today's dancers are young and beautiful, but very different from their predecessors: Nora Kaye, Alicia Alonso, Makarova—you don't forget them when you leave the theater. Toni Lander, the Danish ballerina who partnered with Ivan Nagy, was then also one of the leading dancers.

I signed a contract with a Japanese religious organization called Sokogaku, a popular and powerful sect in Japan. Of course, we would do *Swan Lake* and *Giselle*. What else would they want in Japan?

Before we left the States, I learned that ABT had miscounted the dancers, and one more was needed for *Swan Lake*. Lucia came to me and said, "Paul, I have to engage another dancer." That would of course add to the expense.

"Lucia," I said, "it was so difficult to get this engagement. I am not going to start renegotiating a contract for one dancer. You'll have to pay for it."

"No, that's impossible," she said. Lucia was known to be very stingy.

Finally, I said, "I am sorry. I cannot do anything." Reluctantly, Lucia agreed to pay. When we finally arrived in Japan, there was a huge press conference for the ABT. Lucia became furious because one of the Japanese reporters wanted to know how much of her own money she was investing in the company.

Every week, when we had payday, there was a line leading to the company manager, who handed out the money. And every week, Lucia would line up with the rest of the dancers, so excited that she'd clap her hands together and say, "Goody, goody. Today is payday."

Just what she needed.

One day I had to speak to her about company business and went to her hotel room. I think she had the smallest room in the hotel. It was so small there was barely room in there for the two of us.

"Lucia, why don't you get a bigger room for yourself," I asked.

"Oh, no I couldn't. It's too expensive," she said.

Lucia played the Mother of the Prince in *Swan Lake*. One day we were going to the theater together for a matinee in which she was to perform. In those days it was absolutely impossible to find a Tokyo driver who spoke English. At the entrance to the hotel, we saw a taxi and I asked the doorman to give directions to the theater. The driver said yes to everything, because he did not want to admit that he did not understand a word the doorman said.

Lucia and I got into the back seat. And we drove and we drove and we drove. Soon, there were trees wherever we looked. Clearly, we were somewhere outside of Tokyo, and we didn't have a clue. Neither did the driver. We were lost. When I told the driver to please stop, he didn't understand what I was saying. I gave him the name of the theater, but he just kept on smiling and driving.

Finally, we drove by a police station and we managed to get the driver to stop. Lucia and I did our best to explain that we were lost and needed to get to the theater. Lucia was about to miss the performance, but the only thing she could say was "My God, look at the meter."

"Lucia, who cares? You have to be onstage."

But she was more annoyed about the fare than about the prospect of missing her performance. We got back into the cab with just enough time for Lucia to run out when we got to the theater and change into the costume. The driver was so ashamed of his mistake he refused to take my money.

Toni Lander danced the lead in *Swan Lake* on opening night. I was in the last row because I wanted to see how the stage looked from far back. The performance was wonderful and the audience very enthusiastic. When the curtain opened again, the entire company, led by Toni, lined up for a bow. A few Japanese young ladies in kimonos came out and brought flowers to the dancers. They minced across the stage, handing out bouquets. And everyone started getting one, every last member of the *corps de ballet*, but Toni stood there without so much as a daisy in her hand. Toni kept bowing because she was always expecting a bouquet, but each time another girl shuffled on stage to present flowers she zipped right by Toni. I began to panic, jumped up from my seat, ran backstage, grabbed some flowers, and walked out on stage and handed them to Toni. Everyone in the wings thought either I had either lost my mind or that this was the funniest thing in the world.

One day, we were told that the guru of the Sokogaku organization was coming to see the show. An enormous fleet of limousines brought him and his attendants to the theater. Through an interpreter, he invited Lucia and me to come to his house at another time. We agreed, and a few days later were taken to his palace. We were led into a grand salon, and finally, after we'd been waiting for about a half hour, the doors flew open and the guru entered. He never talked to us directly, but would only address us through an interpreter. Lucia and I sat on either side of him, and when we had finished talking, the three of us posed for a picture. Later on, I told Lucia that we looked like a portrait of God with his archangels. As we were led out, we were told that there were presents for the company; we thanked him very much for the meeting and the gifts, which had been placed in the back of the car while we visited. We drove back to the Imperial Hotel, and there we opened the presents, which we couldn't believe. For the men of the company, there were cases of Coca-Cola, and for the women, cases of ginger ale. Lucia was also given a doll; I was given a statue, which we both thought was so awful that I gave it to the hotel maid at once. Lucia took her doll home.

I also booked ABT in Europe, and on one tour, featuring Carla Fracci, the Italian prima ballerina, as guest star, I took the company to Italy, London, and Santander, Spain, where they were to dance outdoors, on an open stage built in the middle of a huge piazza. The mayor of Santander came to the airport to receive the dancers as part of a welcoming ceremony. Having preceded the company, I waited with him—waited and waited, but the plane filled with dancers did not arrive. Finally, I went to the air traffic control tower, got permission to talk to London, and was told that the chartered plane could not leave, because there was a problem with one of the members of the company.

"What kind of problem?" I asked, expecting the worst.

"One of the musicians is lying down in front of the airplane."

"That's a new one." I had worked with temperamental artists before but never one who did this. The musician, the first violinist, was needed for a Tudor ballet. He had put all his money in his suitcase, and just before the flight was to take off, panicked, and demanded that they fetch his luggage so that he could retrieve his money. Told that this was impossible, he proceeded to lie down in front of the plane. The police were called, but still the violinist wouldn't budge.

At some point the Spanish mayor left the airport, but when he returned the plane was still in London. Finally, after hours and hours of delay, the dancers arrived, without the violinist (a Hungarian, I might add). He was detained in London. Without him, it was impossible to do the Tudor piece, and I was given the job of finding a concert violinist who could perform the following day. I went to the first violinist of the local orchestra, but he refused.

"Oh, no," he said, "this is a concert piece. It will take several days to prepare. I cannot take a chance and ruin my reputation."

"I'll pay you five hundred dollars if you accept," I said.

"Well," he said in a more relaxed tone of voice, "I'll think about it." That did the trick. He accepted the offer and that night, the dancers later told me, they couldn't sleep because the violinist spent the entire time practicing.

The performance was sold out. But disaster struck again. I got a phone call the morning of the performance from the local promoter, informing me that there had been a fire and the rain tarp, the protective covering that would protect the audience in case of rain, had been destroyed.

At the beginning of the performance it started to rain. Luckily the stage was covered, but still it was getting wet, and the dancers in their costumes soaked. The audience was looking for cover anywhere they could. I was extremely worried because I knew that if the rain continued, we would have to make refunds to the audience. However, a standard rule in the contract specified that if the dance started and continued up to the first intermission, the management does not have to return the money to the public. Luckily, the dancers performed until the first intermission, even though the stage was water-logged.

When we went to Verona, Italy, to perform, Carla Fracci, the star, was treated like Pavlova. The company performed *Giselle* at the Coliseum, which attracted an audience of over 20,000 people. It's the most impressive venue for summer theater. Who needs Three Tenors, when you have one dancing diva?

Shortly before the performance was to begin, the stage manager came to me and said we had to announce all changes in the program: those dancers that wouldn't be dancing as well as their replacements. I told him that that wasn't how things were done in America, and besides, no one in the audience would really know or care about changes in the *corps de ballet*. He said it was a union rule and that there would be a penalty if the list wasn't read.

"Well, pay the penalty. Just don't do this or it will be a disaster."

But he wouldn't listen and began to address the audience in English, telling them of all the changes: "Mr. So-and-So will be replaced by another Mr. So-and-So." What a big yawn this was for the audience, as the list went on forever, and nobody understood or cared what was going on. But they had come to see Carla Fracci, and when her name wasn't mentioned they thought she wasn't going to appear. You could feel a lot of tension building in the audience. Suddenly we heard chanting and shouting: "We want Fracci, WE WANT FRACCI!" Soon the whole audience joined in the yelling. It was like a call to revolution! Then Carla's husband, Beppe, ran onto the stage, made a huge gesture with his hands and announced, "La Fracci is going to dance." The whole audience screamed with joy and as they waited for La Fracci to appear, each lit a candle—and 20,000 candles were put out— when the performance started.

Recently, in the fall of 1999, I took American Ballet Theatre to France to dance at one of the most important festivals, "Nouveau Festival International de Danse de Paris," sponsored by Mrs. Jacques Chirac, the President's wife.

Bunraku (Japanese Doll Theater)

In the mid-1960s, I was in Osaka and went to see the Bunraku Doll Theater, the most famous and unique of all puppet companies, dating back to late sixteenth-century Japan. I was interested in all the Japanese arts, not only dance, and also attended performances of Noh plays, Kabuki, and Gagaku.

The ancient Bunraku theater is small and old-fashioned. The puppets are about five feet high, and are manipulated by three handlers, or "doll-actors." Two of the three manipulators wear a black cloak that covers them from head to toe, and black gloves, to give the impression that they are not present. That's the case in many Japanese classical shows, where the one who doesn't want to be seen wears black. The chief manipulator wears the formal town dress of seventeenth-century Kyoto. Many of the Bunraku stories were taken from classical Japanese literature. The manipulators begin their training when they are young. First, they learn how to master the movement of the puppets' feet, which takes about ten years. It takes another decade to master the left arm, and a final ten years to perfect the movement of the right arm and the head. That's thirty years before a manipulator can become an accredited master. When I saw the Bunraku for the first time, it seemed to me the puppets were human. And I thought the Bunraku would have enormous success in America.

I decided I would do the show on my own, acting as producer as well as impresario. The Bunraku is such a historically preeminent company for the Japanese that its managers were very cautious (and very slow) in their negotiations.

I was excited by the idea and when I came back to New York I immediately contacted Lincoln Kirstein, who was, I knew, extremely interested in the arts of the Japanese. He was delighted when he heard my plans, and he showed so much knowledge of the subject, I asked if he would collaborate with me on artistic matters. He agreed to make contact between American Japanese scholars and the management of City Center, where the Bunraku was to perform. More important, he agreed to write the text of the program, on the condition that we guarantee not to allow any advertising to appear in it. Naturally, I agreed because it was so essential that Lincoln be involved.

Lincoln introduced me to Donald Keene, a professor at Columbia University who was an expert in Japanese theater, especially Bunraku. He helped me choose the right repertory for an American audience. He had an enormous collection of photographs of the Bunraku, and Lincoln arranged for us to use many of his photos in the program.

In the history of Japanese theater, first came the Noh plays, then the Bunraku, followed by the Kabuki. As a result, a lot of pieces in the Bunraku repertory were taken over by the Kabuki. But for me the Bunraku remains the most exciting of the different forms of Japanese theater.

In terms of staging, one thing that makes the Bunraku unique is that it does not hang scenery. Instead each piece has a wooden peg that fits into a different hole in the floor. But I knew that would be impossible on a Western stage. I asked Ronald Bates, the stage director of the New York City Ballet, to fly out with me to Hawaii, the first stop on the Bunraku itinerary, to see the construction of the stage there and how it could be applied to the stage at City Center. In Honolulu, the staging was extremely difficult as none of the scenery could be secured. It was just standing on the stage. Suddenly during the performance I attended, I heard an enormous crack. I immediately ran backstage, where the scenery was starting to sway. I was sure at any moment the whole damn thing would collapse. All the stagehands, plus me and Ronnie Bates, had to hold the scenery up until the performance ended.

After Honolulu, I decided that this could not be allowed in New York. It would certainly cause a disaster. Ronnie decided to reconstruct the backdrop so that it could be hung.

Shortly after, we returned to New York. The advance publicity was enormous and we were given eight pages in the Sunday *New York Times Magazine* a week before the 1966 opening. It proved a great boon to ticket sales, and we were soon completely sold out. Before opening night, I asked Lincoln Kirstein how many tickets he needed for his guests. He said, "Paul, you handle your friends and I will handle mine." On opening night, I realized that Donald Keene wasn't in the theater, and it came to light that Lincoln had forgotten to invite him. Keene must have been furious, because the following day I got a letter from his lawyer informing me that I was being sued for having used the photos without permission. In a fright, I called Lincoln and asked him why he hadn't invited Keene. He said, "I made a mistake. I forgot." I then immediately phoned Donald Keene, apologized, and invited him to attend any other performance with his students. After this I went to see Lincoln, who, crazy as usual, said, "Don't worry. I will arrange it."

I waited for Lincoln to take care of it until one day when I met him in the lobby of the New York State Theater. He said he had taken care of it and handed me a piece of paper. "This is my letter to Keene. I hope you approve of it." I was grateful and felt that finally I could breathe a sigh of relief. Then I unfolded the paper and read: "Dear Donald, I think you are right. You should sue Paul Szilard . . ." I almost fainted. I couldn't believe it, but that was typical of Lincoln.

I immediately turned to Morton Baum, former chairman of City Center, explained the situation, and asked for his help. After he read Lincoln's letter, he said, "Are you surprised? Don't you know Lincoln? Don't worry. I will take care of it."

Finally, the director of the Bunraku, who was a good friend of Professor Keene, straightened things out for us and the lawsuit was dropped. I wrote to Keene the next day and offered him tickets to all remaining performances and apologized, again, for the initial oversight.

Clive Barnes was so enthusiastic about the Bunraku that he wrote in his review, "Actors should take lessons from the puppets because they are so human that it could be an example to them."

Thoughts on What Makes an Artist

An artist, in my opinion, has to create something on stage that comes from inside. Even the slightest movement will have a meaning to the audience. For example, I had a great flair for jazz—I think I am a frustrated jazz dancer—and when, just for fun, I improvised for people, I suspect this flair came through in even my tiniest gesture.

People often ask what I think the difference is between dancers today and dancers in my time. When I was a dancer, the most important thing was the dance. We did not have the concern for money that today's dancers do. Their main interests are the union, the contract, their overtime, and their other requirements, all of which take precedence over the dance itself. In my opinion, this makes them more limited dancers. Furthermore, many have a limited knowledge of dance and the other arts, never going to museums or concerts. For instance, the Alvin Ailey American Dance Theater is a household name in America. One of the leading dancers of the New York City Ballet asked not long ago if I could get him tickets to see the Ailey company. I asked him when he last saw them, and he answered, "Never." I don't understand how that's possible. It's not a question of liking or not liking. A dancer needs to know what's going on in the world of which he or she is a part. Mention some famous choreographers and dancers whose names appear regularly in newspapers and magazines, and they've never heard of them. I think this is shocking. It changes the whole outlook of dance. In my day, personality as revealed in performance was extremely important. Today, the average dancer believes that tricks are the most important thing. Though the tricks may be technically marvelous, some extra dimension is lacking.

I see a performance today of a classical ballet company, and I watch their so-called leading stars, and when it's over and I'm back home, I've already forgotten who they are. If you leave a performance and nothing remains with you, then something is wrong. With no personal identity, they all look alike to me.

I consider Anthony Dowell one of the purist classical dancers. When I saw him do *Sleeping Beauty* or any of his signature roles, his approach and artistry were exceptional. Whenever I see other dancers in these roles and don't agree with the way they were performed, I always remember how Dowell did them.

Natalia Makarova was and is unique. I don't see any ballerinas at present who compare with her. For me she is one of the greatest classical ballet dancers. Her nuances, unique. When I saw *Other Dances* on opening night with Natasha and Misha Baryshnikov, it was unforgettable. If I see other dancers performing that ballet, something is always missing.

Among the great dancers I would consider Fred Astaire, because he could do everything—ballet, modern, jazz—and all with such ease, such fantastic feeling, that no other dancer of his entertainment category could compare. Not Gene Kelly, though he was a good dancer. The elegance in Astaire's movement, in the subtleties between his steps was matchless. We classical dancers can feel and see immediately that he was one of us. He was classical, he was modern. I know Misha adored Astaire, and so did Balanchine.

Margot Fonteyn

Margot Fonteyn and I knew each other for years. We liked each other and frequently had lunch or dinner together. Many times she and I even took the same ballet class with Madame Volkova, a very famous Russian ballet teacher, in London, where I saw a lot of Fonteyn's early performances. Even at that time, when I knew much less than I do now, my opinion was that she had a very limited technique. She had some unusual qualities, like the most remarkable back, which is extremely important for certain steps like an arabesque. She really had a swan type of back. But I never considered her the fantastic dancer to whom the whole world later on gave such acclaim. She was a great artist, a great personality, a wonderful performer, but if I compare her today to other artists—to me, Makarova stands on a much higher pedestal.

When Fonteyn was receiving accolades as the greatest ballerina, I felt there was a certain politics involved. Britain needed a national hero, an English prima ballerina assoluta. But in her time there were other great dancers in the Royal Ballet—Violetta Elvin, lesser known but in my opinion a fabulous dancer, or Moira Shearer, who briefly became world-famous starring in the movie *The Red Shoes*. The company never gave them the kind of publicity or push that was lavished on Margot Fonteyn. When I saw Violetta Elvin at the Metropolitan Opera House, I thought the public liked her even better than they did Margot Fonteyn.

Of course, in her personality and artistry, there's no question that Fonteyn was a great dancer. But sometimes a film is shown on television of Margot's early dancing, before she became a partner of Nureyev; I have seen it and cannot believe that she became the great artist that she did. Her technique, her whole approach, seem so limited. But the public always wanted to see her.

I admired Margot as an artist and adored her as a person. She was outspoken, generous in her admiration of other dancers, and honestly self-critical. Once when she was dancing at a Royal Ballet opening night, I was in the wings and saw her make a big jump and fall. On the way backstage she said, "I don't know why I'm doing this ballet, it's not for me."

Rudolf Nureyev

After the Marquis de Cuevas died in 1961, his widow, Margaret Strong, the granddaughter of John D. Rockefeller, lost interest in supporting her late husband's ballet company, "Le Grand Ballet du Marquis de Cuevas." As a result, the company fell apart. Rudolf Nureyev was a member of the company and now was without work. I had been in Paris when, not that long before, Nureyev was performing there with the Kirov and made his decision not to return to the Soviet Union. The French police helped him defect, and for a while he hid in the apartment of Pierre Lacotte, a dancer from the Paris Opera Ballet.

When I learned that the Marquis de Cuevas company still had a contract with Nureyev, the idea of bringing him to the United States crossed my mind. I called the general manager of the Marquis's company in Monte Carlo to discuss the possibility. They were very interested in my taking Nureyev under my wings, and they offered to sell the remainder of his contract— about six months—to me. I was a bit skeptical. It's hard to believe now, but back then nobody outside the dance world had much of a clue as to who Nureyev was, and he certainly wasn't well known in America. Perhaps it was too soon to bring him here. Before I agreed, I told them I needed to find out how much interest there was in this relatively unknown dancer. When I returned home, I immediately contacted the *Bell Telephone Hour* in New York City, at that time the most prominent television venue for music and dance in America. I offered them Nureyev, and their reception was lukewarm. They wanted to know what he could do. "And how much will he cost?"

"Three thousand dollars for Nureyev and a partner," I said, which wasn't an extravagant price for two dancers doing a *pas de deux.*

They declined.

I tried other possibilities, all without success because no one knew who he was. Finally, I phoned Monte Carlo, told them there just wasn't any interest in Rudolf Nureyev at this time, and declined to pick up his contract. That was a big mistake.

Shortly after, I saw Rudolf in Paris, where I had met him many times at the home of Madame Irène Lidova, one of the most prominent dance critics in Europe. But she was more than a critic, because she had been a general manager for Roland Petit, and had worked closely with dancers from the Paris Opera. She is a doyenne of the dance, and is well respected. She still has a mind like a computer and remembers everything. Lidova and I became very close, and even today, I call her a few times a month, and I never leave Paris without a visit to her very small, antique apartment in a very good area of Paris. When you walk in you have the feeling of entering another century. She immediately serves you a glass of vodka. She likes to cook Russian food, and prepares it in a light way when I come for dinner, because she knows I cannot take very heavy cooking. Each time I visit, she greets me with open arms, and over the years we've become as close as family.

When Nureyev was new to the West, he came to depend on Madame Lidova, who was of Russian origin. But though she helped him in many ways, later on he always behaved badly towards her. She had looked after him after he had defected, and the three of us would have dinner together and talk about the dance and theater. Rudi was personable and simple at that time.

But later, when he became very famous, he hardly greeted her. He became extremely arrogant. Irène told me she was shocked by his behavior, shocked that he had forgotten all that she had done for him. But I've heard this from others, too. He was not known as a very kind person. I'm sure he had his close friends, but my impression was that as he became more and more famous, his egotism got progressively worse. I called him a muzsik (peasant). I dislike people who have bad manners. Rudolf and I always had an amicable relationship but we never became close friends. I admired him as an artist, even though I found him anti-musical. When he couldn't dance anymore, he did some conducting. I couldn't believe that someone so unmusical would become a conductor.

I found his life tragic because an artist should have the self-knowledge and critical insight to know how long he should go on dancing. I stopped dancing when I felt they were about to start throwing tomatoes. Evidently, he never had that sense. In my opinion, he should have stopped dancing fifteen years before he at last retired. Those final years he could barely move. But the public loved seeing a star, and were happy to pay the price to do so. Actually, it was Nureyev who paid the ultimate price. He had an enormous personality and stage presence, but technique wise, I always thought Baryshnikov was the stronger dancer. I did admire Nureyev for being an autodidact. He studied, he read, he learned languages, he collected art, though I found some of his collection mediocre; evidently here, too, his critical judgment was not strong enough.

"Rudi," I said to him once at Lidova's apartment, "I might be able to take you to America, but first you have to sign a managerial contract with me."

"Contract? Why?" He had no idea what I was talking about.

The Soviets didn't have individual managerial contracts. Artists signed only with a company.

But unable to generate any real interest in having Rudi perform, I quietly gave up on the idea. Too bad. I think he could have gone places!

In Paris, many artists hung out in the coffee houses of St. Germain des Près. Once, on my way to Café de Flor, which became almost like my headquarters whenever I was in Paris, I ran into a beautiful young German boy, a hustler, whom I used to pass all the time on his favorite street corner. We'd always speak to each other in German. One day, we were talking when Rudolf started walking towards us. Clearly, it wasn't me he was interested in because many times he'd pass me without so much as a nod. Today, apparently, was different.

"Hello, Paul. How are you?" He was beaming.

Of course, he wasn't looking at me at all.

We talked for a few minutes longer before Rudi realized he wouldn't be able to make a pick-up. When he was gone I said to the young man, "That was Nureyev. Do you know him?"

"Do I know him?" he said, "I've met him many times under the bridge, and he's a bitch. He wants it free. He always wants to pay very little."

Pas de Quatre (for the Bell Telephone Hour)

In the mid-1960s, I had the idea to present the famous ballet *Pas de Quatre*. It was a great opportunity to have four major stars dance together. I knew the television people would be thrilled by the idea of having all those famous dancers on the same program. And when I brought my idea to the *Bell Telephone Hour*, the reaction was as I had expected. My plan was to get the reigning stars of the ballet to participate. To do this, I asked for a lot of money, which nobody seemed to mind. The *Telephone Hour* had backers who were immediately interested in the project.

The original *Pas de Quatre* premiered in London in 1845 with the prima ballerinas of the time: Maria Taglioni, Carlotta Grisi,

Fanny Cerrito, and Lucile Grahn. Jules Perrot was the chore-ographer. They say it took a lot of hard work on the part of the director of the theater, Benjamin Lumley, to get the four stars together. From my experiences, I'd say that was an understate-ment. I'm sure those divas wore him out.

Our ballet was choreographed by Anton Dolin, the versatile British dancer and choreographer, whom we lovingly referred to as Pat, and to stage the dance he directed me to Celli, the ballet master in New York, who had studied with Enrico Cecchetti. Ali-cia Markova, Mia Slavenska, and Dolin himself all studied with Celli. Pat said, "Paul, you and Celli will put on the ballet because you both know my choreography." My goal was to have Alicia Alonso, Maria Tallchief, Nora Kaye, and Mia Slavenska as the stars. The part Taglioni had danced is the lead. So I went about hiring the number one dancer, and that led me right to Alicia Alonso, who was then in Cuba. She was delighted to be offered the role and accepted graciously.

Maria Tallchief, in Chicago at this time, was my next call. Maria said "yes," but only if she could dance the lead.

I began to have the same problems they had one hundred and fifty years ago, when *Pas de Quatre* premiered, namely, publicity and billing. When Maria heard that I had offered the lead to Ali-cia she said, "Paul, when I dance, I have to be number one. I am the prima ballerina of America."

"Maria, that's always been her part. Her whole life she's danced Taglioni," I said.

"I don't care. If that's the case, then I'm not interested."

"OK, Maria. Let me ask Alicia if she will take second billing." So I left off these negotiations and called Alicia in Cuba. I told her about Maria's feelings about Taglioni.

"What?" Alicia said. "She doesn't want to get second? She was in the *corps de ballet* when I was already a star!"

"Alicia," I said, "you have to understand that she's an American ballerina . . . ," but she cut me off before I could finish my sentence.

"Then I'm not interested."

After that, I went back to Maria, deciding that she would be

Taglioni. Then came more questions about billing and publicity. I spoke to the production director at the *Telephone Hour* and we decided that we would set all the women's names in a circle, so that they would all appear equal. Since none of the dancers liked this very much, I then came up with something new that I presented to Maria.

"Maria, the billing will be two lines. On the first line will be Alicia Alonso and Maria Tallchief. And on the second line will be Nora Kaye and Mia Slavenska."

"And who is going to be the first on the first line?" Maria asked.

"What's the difference?" I said.

"Listen, Paul," she said, "you have spent too much time in Japan and are starting to read backwards. You read it the Japanese way, and I read it the American way." We both burst out laughing. But in the end Maria and I could not come to an agreement. In her place I engaged Melissa Hayden of the New York City Ballet.

During rehearsals, the dancers argued among themselves a lot. Each remembered the steps her own way, and they all had to be constantly reminded that we were using Dolin's choreography. To make matters worse, Alicia, Nora, and Melissa were always picking on Mia. I don't know if they were jealous, but nasty remarks about her were flying around the room. Slavenska, who was a very strong worker, seemed to take it in stride. She let nothing get in the way of her performance.

Within a month, we held a general rehearsal in a television studio on Columbus Circle, and invited the backers and sponsors from the *Telephone Hour*. They wanted to see where their money was going. It was a terrible day, raining and snowing. Everyone came in with wet shoes and coats, leaving their open umbrellas outside the studio to dry. Once they had taken their seats, the backers waited for the glamorous ballerinas to arrive. At least, that's what they thought. The backers had imagined all the dancers would look like Marilyn Monroe when they walked through the door, so there were a few gasps after Nora shook out her wet umbrella and stood there disheveled. She looked like a bag lady in a big overcoat, boots, a sweater pulled down to her knees, and no makeup. The backers, in shock, looked as if they were having second thoughts.

Mia Slavenska walked in next, wearing a mink coat. She always paid great attention to her looks and was very chic and sophisticated, though it didn't take much to look glamorous after the soggy Nora Kaye. Mia was followed by her publicity agent and a few other members of her entourage. I was happy that somebody was looking good.

Alicia arrived next with an entourage of four people, all speaking Spanish. By this time, she had a serious problem with her eyesight and needed somebody to walk with her. This became a problem when we started to rehearse, even though she knew *Pas de Quatre* in her sleep, having danced it so many times.

The last one to arrive, with her large, bright smile and her harsh voice, was Melissa Hayden.

Once all the dancers were in the studio and had changed into their costumes, Ralph Bellamy, from Hollywood, who served as the narrator, could introduce each ballerina as part of the ballet. He announced, "Ladies and gentlemen, now you are going to see the century's greatest ballerinas. Miss Nora Kaye, the prima ballerina of New York City Ballet and American Ballet Theatre." There was applause as Nora walked in and took her place.

"And now, ladies and gentleman, Miss Melissa Hayden of the New York City Ballet." Again, more applause as Melissa entered the stage.

"And now, presenting Miss Alicia Alonso, the distinguished ballerina of Cuba."

Alicia called me over immediately and said, "Paul, I don't like what he's saying about me."

"Why?" I asked.

"I don't like that word. Tell him to change it." She couldn't pronounce distinguished.

"Why, what's wrong with it?" I asked.

"I don't like it. I don't want it," she said.

"Do you know what it means?"

"No. I don't know what it means, but I don't like it."

"All right," I said, "We'll change it."

This was about the third or fourth time that Bellamy had had to change his speech, and he was growing impatient. None of the dancers liked what had been written, and he was left with a changed script after each introduction.

One part of the ballet, originally danced by Cerrito, has demanding footwork, and none of the dancers wanted to attempt it. I was absolutely beside myself and not knowing exactly what to do, I turned to Nora first.

"I don't want to do it, Paul. I'm tired. I don't want to jump so much," she said.

"Nora," I said, raising my voice, "I'll give you five hundred dollars extra if you'll do it."

"Of course, darling, I'm going to do it," she purred.

When the early rehearsals were completed, it was time to get into costumes. As Mia Slavenska had a little ballet company, in Los Angeles, with *Pas de Quatre* in its repertory, we rented those costumes. They were waiting for us in Brooklyn, where we were to perform the ballet. When we got there, on a Sunday, Mia quickly put on her own costume. It was more elaborate than the others, with more tulle skirts. Alicia was furious.

She said, "Look at our costumes, they're awful. And look at hers. Tell her to remove one skirt from her dress, so it becomes as flat as ours, or I won't go out in mine." I promised to arrange it, but I never said a word to Mia. I figured once the ballet began it would be too late for Alicia to object.

Next we had a problem with the flowers they all wore in their hair. Alicia called me to her dressing room.

"Paul, I don't like these flowers."

"Why? What's wrong with them?"

"They're too small. I want it bigger."

"But darling," I said, "taping begins in ten minutes."

"I don't care. I must have it."

"Alicia, it's Sunday. Where do you want me to get the flowers?"

"You find it, or I don't do it, darling. It's very simple."

The stage manager and I somehow found flowers in the costume shop. And then the full rehearsal began. In accordance with the choreography, the ballerinas enter the stage, one after the other, and form a line, while holding their very classical poses. Alicia entered first, made a circle, then held her pose. Melissa and Nora followed, keeping their circles tight. When Mia entered, she made a huge circle, much bigger than the others, before joining the other women in the line. Nora came out of her classical, angelic pose and said to me, "Tell her to cut short that circle. Who does she think we are, chorus girls?" She then resumed her eighteenth-century stance. Nora could look like a dancer from long ago, but she certainly could never sound like one!

During the performance, we had to make accommodations for Alicia because of her failing vision. Signs in those colors she could see were placed on the stage to mark her exits and her entrances. In each wing, we had people waiting for her. If after she exited she needed to get to the other side of the stage, a stagehand would carry her there in time for her next entrance.

During rehearsals we faced another problem in that Nora was also rehearsing at the time with American Ballet Theatre. It seemed that when Alicia came to New York to dance *Pas de Quatre*, Ballet Theatre was invited to perform in Cuba.

One day Nora called me and said, "Paul, darling, I know you are going to kill me, but I can't do the Telephone Hour because Lucia needs me."

"Nora," I said, "Are you out of your mind? You signed a contract."

"I know. What do you want me to do? We're going to Cuba and they need me for *Fall River Legend*." That was of course Agnes de Mille's signature ballet.

"Nora, it is out of the question. You signed a contract. I signed with *The Bell Telephone Hour*. I don't care how you do it, but you'll have big problems. I'll sue you."

"Do whatever you want Paul, I can't help it," she said.

"Yes, you can. Go tell Lucia that you have another engagement."

"Well, I'll see what I can do."

ABT was ready to fly to Cuba. The company was at the airport in New York, and, I heard, Nora was with them. The Cuban plane they had to take was being repaired while they waited. There were plane parts on the tarmac, and mechanics working on the plane's engines. Well, everyone knew Nora was afraid of flying, and some of the dancers decided to tease her. "Look, Nora. They're just putting the plane together now." She took one look at the loose parts on the tarmac and said, "I am not going." Too terrified to board the plane, she found Lucia Chase and told her, "I hurt my foot and I cannot go." There was nothing Lucia could do. Nora returned to her apartment, American Ballet Theatre left for Cuba without her, and she fulfilled her commitment to me.

On the day of the *Telephone Hour* telecast, all the dancers, American and Cuban, wanted to watch Alicia in *Pas de Quatre*, so a TV was placed in the dressing room of the theater in Havana. Everybody from American Ballet Theatre, including Lucia Chase, was watching the show, when Nora came out and danced. Not to mention that her role required the most leaps. After telling Lucia she had a bad foot, there she was dancing *Pas de Quatre*. I was told that Lucia became hysterical. She didn't talk to me for quite a while after that because of course she blamed me for everything.

Unsuccessful Negotiations: Lily Pons, Leopold Stokowski, Marlene Dietrich

In the 1960s I wanted to book Lily Pons, the coloratura soprano, who at the time was married to André Kostelanetz, the conductor. They had an unbelievable apartment in New York, overlooking the East River and filled with fabulous paintings. When I offered her the opportunity to sing in Japan, she seemed very interested. But during negotiations she told me that she would go for only one week and wouldn't sing more than twice.

"Twice?" I couldn't believe it. It would cost a fortune for us to travel to Asia, particularly with her own entourage—flutist, secretary, manager, and makeup woman— all flying first class—and we'd never make enough money giving only two concerts.

I tried to explain all this to her, but she had other things on her mind.

"I can't sing more than twice," she said, "Because I will be very busy in Tokyo."

"What *else* will you be doing in Tokyo?" I asked.

"I just bought a house in California and I want to make it Oriental, so I have a lot of furniture to buy. I will be very busy, and won't have time to sing more."

That was the end of that. We never were able to come to an agreement.

My contact in Japan asked for Leopold Stokowski to come and conduct their symphony orchestra. I talked to the maestro and he responded quite favorably. His financial conditions were acceptable. However, he wouldn't fly. He needed to travel by sea with an entourage that included his two grandchildren and their nurse.

"Do we have to pay for them?" I asked.

"Of course," he said.

"Maestro," I said, "With all due respect, why should we pay for the grandchildren and their nurse?"

"Because they've never been to Japan," he answered, effectively ending that negotiation.

A contact of mine in Germany asked if I could arrange to have Marlene Dietrich perform there, doing the same act she had performed in Australia, wearing her famous white sequin dress and fox coat. I immediately called her agent in Hollywood, and we started our negotiations. Though he asked for a fortune, all was going well, until one day the telephone rang. I picked up the phone and a gravelly voice said hello.

"Who is this?" I asked.

"Marlene Dietrich," she answered.

I was not sure I heard her correctly.

"Who?" I asked again.

"Marlene Dietrich. I would like to speak to Mr. Szilard."

"That's me." I couldn't believe that she personally was on the phone.

"You're the one who wants to bring me to Berlin? I would like to discuss all the conditions."

"But I've already talked to your agent about this."

"I don't care," she said, "because I don't trust him. I want to hear it myself."

Among her demands: "I want a limousine to be on the tarmac when I come out of the plane. [She would not go inside the airport.] And I want four bodyguards. One to be outside the door to my hotel room, two at the theater, and one close to me at all times. Plus I'll be coming with my secretary, my hairdresser, and my makeup person." And so on and so on.

I thought there'd be more people in her entourage than there would be in the audience.

"Also, I don't want any newspapermen waiting for me. I will do no interviews. I will go right to my hotel room, and then to the theater to perform."

"Miss Dietrich, how do you want us to make publicity if you won't give permission for photographs and interviews?"

"No publicity," she said. "Find another way. If you need it, then I'm not interested."

Then she wanted to talk about the financial details. Her agent and I had previously agreed on her fee, which was huge and was to be placed in an escrow account.

"What?" she said.

I told her again.

"That is absolutely out of the question. I don't know what you mean by escrow, but it's absolutely out of the question. I want it in cash." She had no idea what escrow was, and, interestingly enough, the French word for crook is pronounced very similarly to the English escrow. She must have found the whole conversation absurd.

Just a few months earlier, she had fallen into the orchestra pit when she was performing in Australia. She wasn't a young chicken anymore, and no one would pay her in cash. It was too much of a risk.

Then I learned Dietrich had reason to be scared. Personal threats against her had been made in Germany and people there were threatening to bomb the theater, because she had been anti-Hitler (and pro-American) during the war.

When I told her daughter, Maria Riva, of Dietrich's demands, she was furious and said, "Oh, that crazy woman. She should be happy to get some money. She hasn't got a penny to her name."

"So why don't you talk to her?" I said. "She's your mother."

"It won't do any good if I talk to her. That crazy woman! She needs the money."

Some Choreographers and a Composer

I was a classically trained ballet dancer, but I choreographed many pieces not in the classical idiom. I was a great admirer, always, of modern dance. When I came to America, I was overwhelmed the first time I saw Martha Graham and her work. I still think that in our time no one has equaled the height of her artistic achievement. Who can even come close? The prominent choreographers today were all influenced by Martha Graham—many, indeed, came right out of her school and her company—and to me, all of them have to stand in line behind her.

Merce Cunningham had been the second man to join Graham's company, following Erick Hawkins. Merce was a wonderful classical ballet dancer. He stayed with Graham for many years, then left to make his own choreography. When he first started, I couldn't understand how anybody could like what he was doing. Rumor had it that half the audience went home at the first intermission, and when the remaining half began to throw chairs, the dancers would say, "What a fantastic success!" Now, I look at Merce's work with a completely different eye and realize that I should have accepted it earlier. I must have improved in learning how to watch and understand modern dance.

Many years ago I sailed to Europe on the Queen Mary and Merce and composer John Cage happened to be on board as well. I was never very fond of Cage's music, and during the course of a conversation I said to him, "Listen, John, why do you ruin the piano? In a three-hour concert, you put in toilet paper and chopsticks and whatever else you can find. If you don't like the piano, why don't you construct a new instrument?" He just smiled and changed the subject.

I knew Jerry Robbins very well because we took classes together at the very beginning. Jerry was a wonderful dancer. I always liked him very much as a performer. When he was onstage, he was exceptional, with a very good technique. When he started to make choreography, I immediately felt that this was going to be something for the future—not just for classical ballet or modern dance, but for the Broadway stage as well. Jerry was one of the great choreographers of our time.

I'm truly sorry that Michael Kidd no longer choreographs. I still remember when he did *On Stage* for American Ballet Theatre in 1945. It was something of a novelty, in that the setting was a backstage area, but the unusual choreography was what made it memorable. When Michael went on to do Broadway shows and movies, his dances were exceptional. I consider him a major choreographer.

PART V

ALVIN AILEY,
JUDITH JAMISON,
AND TODAY

As I WORKED WITH BLACK MODERN COMPANIES like Alvin
Ailey, I always sensed that the warm feeling I got from them
was so much more than I got from any white company. I've handled a lot of dance companies: the only one that really has a feeling of humanity is, for me, the Ailey company. That's one of the
reasons I became extremely interested in working with them.
When I go backstage to see the Ailey company, the dancers come
to embrace me and kiss me—we have a deep, personal contact.
Why have they had such enormous success on stage? Because they
have the same kind of contact with the public. They become as
one with the audience. I don't mean to imply that the classical
companies practice discrimination—they don't at all—but there is
a certain iron curtain between "we" and the "other." They are
cold. I don't feel any warmth from them. If I drop in on any of the
major classical ballet companies which have been under my management, they casually say, "Hi, how are you"—but it's very su-
perficial. At their offices or on the stages where they are rehearsing they barely greet me. They convey the same attitude in
performance. Very few classical dancers have the warm connection with the audience that black dancers have.

Who has that warmth today among classical dancers?
Natasha Makarova. I feel she has a heart and likes to reach out
to people. She is a gracious, wonderful human being. But most
dancers are so egocentric they don't see anything around them.

If you talk to young dancers today, it's always about *them*, what *they* dance, what *they* should do.

Alvin Ailey was of course a dedicated fighter for his race and I admired him for that. He also probably liked me—though he never told me this—in part because he recognized that I shared his feelings for the cause. I'm sure it brought us closer.

Alvin Ailey

One evening, after the Alvin Ailey American Dance Theater performed in Taiwan, Alvin and I were walking the streets that were teeming with life even at such a late hour. The weather was mild, and we were both in good spirits after the company had given a triumphant performance.

We wandered through the city, found ourselves in the red-light district, and stopped in front of the glowing neon sign of a striptease club. A billboard in front of the entrance read, "Miss Lolita, Egyptian dancer, descendant of Moses," and showed a photograph of a naked girl with bleached blonde hair that seemed as long as the Nile—it fell from her head to the floor.

Well, when Alvin read that, his eyes lit up, as if this were the most fantastic thing in the world. He insisted that we go in. "Paul," he said and laughed, "I have to see that because I need new steps for my ballet."

So we paid our admission and entered, sat down at a small table in front of the stage, and ordered drinks. A few minutes later, the lights dimmed, and the star entered the stage from behind some silver streamers. A drum roll was followed by music that sounded as if it came from the soundtrack of a bad harem movie.

The dancer wore nothing but tassels and a G-string, and was incredibly busty. Enormous. It seemed she had bosoms everywhere. And she was able to manipulate those tassels with enviable skill. They'd fly up or drop down, move in circles to the left, or back to the right. You could get dizzy trying to keep up with her.

Alvin was in heaven. "I've never seen anything like it," he said.

When it was time to leave, Alvin was glowing. "I think I'm ready to get back to the dance studio and work. I got my steps," he said.

"Alvin, please do me one favor. Just make sure you don't change the choreography for *Revelations*."

"I promise," he said, laughing, "I promise."

Alvin and I were best friends for about thirty years. That's also how long I've been impresario for the Alvin Ailey American Dance Theater, the company he founded in 1958. When I first saw them in the mid-1960s, I recognized the dancers were talented and Alvin's choreography was important. Nonetheless, when company manager Ivy Clarke asked if I wanted to represent them, I refused. I didn't feel I wanted to take them on, not just yet. To be honest, I didn't care very much for the company at that time. I thought they had not quite developed their own style, and also they were quite small, with no more than fifteen to eighteen dancers, which was a limiting factor for me in terms of repertoire and bookings.

I remember being in Geneva, Switzerland, when the Ailey company was performing. Alvin was still dancing at that time, and he was thrilling to watch—a gorgeous dancer. After the performance, I went backstage, and Alvin suggested that we go out to dinner. He then asked me to take the company under my wings, but I told him what I had previously told Ivy, that it wasn't the right time. I felt the company lacked direction. It was jazz. It was modern. Stylistically, I thought it was a mishmosh. I wanted to be the impresario when it truly felt like Alvin's company.

"Alvin," I said, "I am very interested in your company, but let's wait until I feel you have your own style. Call me then, and we'll come together."

I had completely forgotten this conversation until Alvin reminded me of it many years later, when we were in Cannes, and had become close friends. "You know," he said, "I will never forget what you told me in Geneva. You told me that I didn't have my own definite style. And I like that you said it. I've never forgotten it."

Later on, Ivy Clarke called me again, when the company was in a very bad financial situation and needed to tour. She had managed to get the company booked into the Brooklyn Academy of Music, an important venue for the arts. That was typical Ivy Clarke. She was an amazing woman, taking care of the company, and also of Alvin. After Brooklyn, the company gained new recognition, became very successful, and soon after were engaged to dance at a Broadway theater. The company finally had an identity and was coming into their own, and that's when I felt it was time to represent them.

I got them an engagement at the Sadler's Wells Theatre in London, where they were a huge success. The guarantee I negotiated was about three times more than they had ever received. Ailey and I made a contract naming me the exclusive manager of the company for all overseas performances.

As they became more and more successful, I was of course able to get them more and more money. In the meantime, Alvin and I established the strong personal friendship that lasted until the day he died. We met privately, or we'd go out to dinner with friends. He'd come to my house, but, interestingly, he never had me—or anyone—over to his. In nearly thirty years, he never let me into any of his apartments. I knew that he was very disorderly and untidy and didn't want me to see his mess.

Alvin always asked me to go with him on vacations. We went to the south of France, to Morocco, to Greece, and to many other places together. We even went to a spa in New Mexico to lose weight. No matter what we did, we always had a wonderful time. One time in Morocco, we rented separate bungalows on the beach. That's when I first noticed Alvin's habits. Though he never had people to his home, he had plenty of new friends to the bungalow. But I could tell that most of these people were befriending Alvin in order to supply him with drugs. We never talked about it. I felt it wasn't my business to ask about it, and he never volunteered anything.

In New York, we phoned each other almost every morning at ten o'clock. I always believed that Alvin felt free to speak his mind with me, whether it be about a professional or a personal matter. Though I was on the business side of the company, he knew that I had a strong background in dance, plus solid artistic judgment. He and I often had different opinions, which pleased Alvin, because he liked to hear other suggestions, even if he ended up doing exactly what he wanted. Many times we'd hang up on each other, or Alvin would shout, "Well, why don't you take the whole damn company and do with them what you want."

"I won't do it, because it's your company, not mine," I'd reply.

Though we argued and argued, our friendship stayed strong until the end of his life. Alvin was an exceptional man whose personality was larger than life, both on and off the stage.

Alvin was a good choreographer but an uneven one. Of course, *Revelations* is a masterpiece, and many of his other ballets are quite good, but others simply do not measure up. I think Alvin himself was pretty clear about his abilities as a choreographer and was clever enough to recognize that many times his choreography was limited. He did several ballets that he hated afterward, saying, "This has to go."

He showed that he knew his weaknesses by frequently making a joke like, "Paul, let's go to the ballet. I need some steps for my next dance." Though this was a joke that might have contained an element of truth, in fact his greatness was that in the main he did not copy anybody else's style. All his ballets were Ailey through and through. You can watch performances of modern dance companies today and see the influence of Martha Graham, or of Jerry Robbins, or of Merce Cunningham. You don't have that feeling with Alvin. Good or bad, Alvin is Alvin.

We always sat together on opening night. If there was a ballet I didn't like, I'd look at him in a certain way, and he'd know exactly what I meant. "You're right," he'd say, "that must go." Or "Well, we'll just have to play it a couple of times because we got money for it from backers."

In the early days, Alvin had fabulous dancers in his company, including Judith Jamison, Sara Yarborough, Donna Wood, Clive

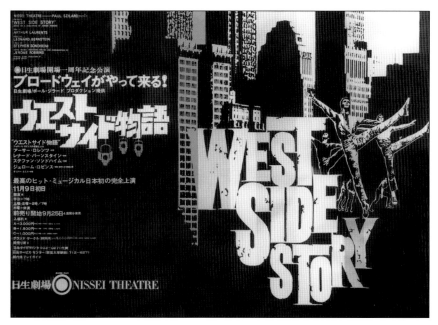

One of the first Broadway productions ever to appear in Tokyo, Japan.
Produced by Paul Szilard.

Credits for *West Side Story*.

Mario, star of the
Dancers of Bali.

Eunsun Jun is
Universal Ballet's
Shim Chung.

Photo: Kwan-Jin Chung

Star Performer of the Bunraku Puppet Theater. Kyoto, Japan.

TEMPORADA OFICIAL DE BAILADOS

(a ser realizada entre 27 de Setembro e 27 de Novembro, dividida em dois periodos)

1.º Periodo: de 27 de Setembro até 16 de Outubro

O Coreógrafo

PAUL SZILARD,

com os

Primeiros Bailarinos

ISTVAN RABOWSKY e NORA KOVACH

e TATIANA GRANTZEVA

Primeira Bailarina do "Metropolitan OPERA HOUSE"

e JACK BEABER

do "Ballet Theatre"

Repertório :

AS SILFIDES, música de Chopin — UIRAPURU, de Vil-la-Lobos — DOM QUIXOTE (Pas-de-deux), de Minkus — SHEERAZADE, de Rimsk-Korsakow — COPELIA, de Deli-bes — COMPOSIÇÃO ABSTRATA, de Vivaldi-Bach — (Or-questração de Francisco Mignone — PAS-DE-DEUX, de Tchaikowsky — O ETERNO TRIANGULO, de Ribailowsky — SALOMÉ de Richard Strauss — BALLET ACADEMY, de J. Enesco — O ESPECTRO DA ROSA, de Weber — ESME-RALDA, de Pugni — MASCARADE, de Katchaturian.

2.º Periodo: de 7 até 27 de Novembro

O Coreógrafo

LEONIDE MASSINE

com os

Primeiros Bailarinos

MARIA TALLCHIEFF

e ANDRÉ EGLEWSKY

Repertório :

O LAGO DOS CISNES, música de Tchaikowsky — QUA-DROS NUMA EXPOSIÇÃO, de Mussorgsky — GAÎTÉ PARI-SIENNE, de Offembach, Coreografia de Massine — BODAS DE AURORA, de Tchaikowsky — OS SETE PECADOS, de Ravel — PAQUITA, de Minkus — RAPSODIA BRASILEIRA de Francisco Mignone, ou SÃO FRANCISCO DE ASSIS, de Paul Hindemith, (Careografica de Massine — O TRICORNIO, de De Falla (Coreografia de Massine) — O CISNE NEGRO, de Tchaikowysky — DOM QUIXOTE, de Minkus — RHAPSO-DY IN BLUE, de Gershwin — SYLVIE, de Delibes.

Official poster announcing the guest choreographers,
Paul Szilard and Léonide Massine, at the
Municipal Opera House, Rio de Janeiro, Brazil.

Photo: Henri SouMireu–Lartigue

Gala at the Bolshoi Opera House in Moscow, with Merrill Ashley
between her husband and Yuri Grigorovich.

Party for Alexandra Danilova with, to her right,
Jack Anderson and Suki Schorer.

With Natasha Makarova and Vladimir Malakov at
American Ballet Theatre Gala in New York City.

With Alvin Ailey in Tokyo, Japan.

With Patrick
Dupond in
dressing room.

To Paul Szilard
    With best wishes,   Ronald Reagan

At the White House reception when Alvin Ailey received the
1988 Kennedy Center Award, with President Ronald Reagan.

Allegra Kent in George Balanchine's *Seven Deadly Sins*,
New York City Ballet (1958).

(Photo: © Fred Fehl—Courtesy Allegra Kent Collection)

The official poster celebrating two of the greatest dancers in the world.

(Photo: Courtesy Alvin Ailey American Dance Theater)

Alvin Ailey American Dance Theater Opening Night Gala,
with Oprah Winfrey and Donna Wood.

Rehearsal at Paris Opera House. Alvin Ailey and Ulysses Dove.

Photo: Francette Levieux

Photo: Francette Levieux

Alvin Ailey in Paris.

With Desmond Richardson, star of Alvin Ailey
American Dance Theater.

Patrick Dupond,
star of the Paris
Opera Ballet, in
Alvin Ailey's
Precipice.

Photo: Francette Levieux

With Mme. Chirac, wife of French President, at the 1999 Opening
Gala of American Ballet Theatre in Paris, with Julie Kent to her right.

Reception at the White House with President and
Mrs. Clinton, in honor of Judith Jamison receiving the
Kennedy Center Award, November 1999.

Judi—the love of my life.

Judith Jamison and Violette Verdy saluting me at my 25th Anniversary as impresario for Alvin Ailey American Dance Theater.

"To Paul Szilard—in homage—H. Matisse." A gift from the artist— a signed copy of his book of sketches.

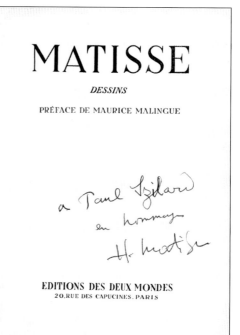

MATISSE

DESSINS

PRÉFACE DE MAURICE MALINGUE

*a Paul Szilard
en hommage
H. Matisse*

EDITIONS DES DEUX MONDES
20, RUE DES CAPUCINES, PARIS

Thompson, Mari Kajiwara, and Masazumi Chaya. In addition to being great dancers, they all had powerful personalities. It's always been my belief that on stage it's not enough to have wonderful technique. You've got to bring something more to the performance if you're going to be considered an artist. Personality is what makes you different from other dancers. It's what makes you a star.

Alvin himself had plenty of personality. He also had an incredible sense of theatricality. He was a man for the theater, which he knew in and out. No matter what he did, it always *looked* good, whether I liked it or not. I often questioned his taste when it came to design and costumes, and sometimes I even differed with him on choreography: I sometimes saw movement in dance differently than he did.

I don't agree with the French mentality and think they have things backwards when it comes to modern dance. A well-known newspaper woman interviewed Alvin in Paris, and though he spoke French, I came with him on the interview since my French was better. The interviewer was talking about choreography in general and how it should express something very deep and philosophical. She asked, "Mr. Ailey, what do you want to express when you are choreographing a ballet?" Alvin didn't miss a beat and said, "Nothing."

She was flabbergasted.

"All I want is that the public should like my ballet, and if they enjoy it, then I am very happy," he added. She had expected to hear about Schopenhauer and Sartre, but Alvin told the truth instead. I admired Alvin very much for his honesty.

Of course, I understood that his apparently glib reply had much deeper meaning. Yes, it is true he used to say that dance should educate as well as entertain, and he was always concerned about its connection to his African-American heritage. But in Alvin's opinion, as well as mine, when you dance, *dance*. When Maurice Béjart explains a new ballet, you feel as if you need a Ph.D. in philosophy to understand what he is saying.

Alvin had many exceptional qualities, and I always admired the pride he took in being who he was. He was very good friends with the expatriate writer James Baldwin, who then lived on the Riviera. When Alvin and I were in Paris, James would come up from the south of France and we'd discuss racial discrimination and how it affected the art world. Alvin got disgusted when he saw that people of color could not advance or were not properly accepted within their fields. Alvin's intense concern for equal rights helped to develop the fighter in me and made me want to work even harder for the company.

Alvin told me that the greatest inspiration for him as a choreographer was Judith Jamison. He felt that Judi could bring his ideas to life, and he was energized by working with her. At the same time, he admitted the negative feelings he sometimes had for her because she was so difficult. She always challenged him. With one look, she could tell him that something was not right with the choreography. She did not accept every move, every step immediately, and that made Alvin nervous. He'd call me and say, "I hate to work with her, but what can I do? She's the only one who excites my imagination."

There was a period of several months when Alvin and Judi did not talk to each other. I thought it was unthinkable to tour the company around the world with the founder and artistic director not talking to its star. They would pass each other backstage as if they were strangers. I decided finally that I had to bring them back together. I called Judi and said, "Judi, I'm going to arrange it that you meet Alvin and clear up this situation." And then I went to Alvin and said, "This cannot work, because you have to make ballets, and basically you two love each other, and the whole situation has gotten out of hand." Of course, neither of them would listen to me at first.

But, one day, when we were in a theater in Berlin, I arranged for them to meet during a rehearsal. They started talking, and after a short time, they gradually began to communicate and to become very good friends once again.

Alvin adored Katherine Dunham, and felt that she should be

treated with the same reverence as Martha Graham or Agnes de Mille. He thought she was one of the great dancer/choreographers and deserved to be honored for that. In the 1980s the Ailey company was invited to perform at the Palais des Sports in Paris, and the director asked for something special. Alvin suggested a Dunham evening.

Alvin came to me for my opinion. I hadn't had any contact with Dunham since my teaching days at her school many years earlier. But as an impresario I was honestly against Alvin's idea. It was already thirty years since the height of Dunham's popularity. I felt that by this time most people in Europe had, unfortunately, forgotten about Dunham, and that it would be difficult for such an event to fill the house in the enormous Palais des Sports. But Alvin insisted on offering a program of her work. We had many arguments about this, which usually ended up with my telling him that the generation that admired and attended Dunham's concerts just didn't exist anymore.

"Alvin," I said, "you know where you should put this show? In the cemetery. Because those people who know the Katherine Dunham troupe are already there." But that only made Alvin more insistent that she receive his homage. I continued to argue but Alvin wouldn't budge, and finally we put the Dunham production on the Ailey company's rehearsal schedule.

It turned out to be just as I had predicted: a nightmare. The rehearsals brought new demands every minute: get this, get that. But Alvin didn't give a damn and spent whatever money he had available. When he arranged for Dunham to have the best luxury hotel and a limousine available to her twenty-four hours a day, I could see he was following a recipe for disaster.

The director of the Palais des Sports came to me in New York, very negative about what he had already seen. He told me he was quite concerned that the Dunham work chosen would not do well in Paris, which has a very sophisticated dance audience.

One day Miss Dunham called and asked me to approach Cardin or St. Laurent and tell them that she would gladly wear one of their creations on opening night. Luckily, later she called again and said, "Paul, don't worry about the dress. I'm having one made by a wonderful designer in Chicago."

The costumes and the scenery were extraordinarily expensive but the ballet was not a success. Mediocre, at best, it was panned by the critics, who wrote that the work may have succeeded thirty years ago but now was terribly dated. It was a total flop at the box office, and for years afterward, the Palais des Sports director wanted nothing to do with Alvin Ailey. I recall the company lost about $400,000, which in those days was an enormous amount of money.

In another visit to Paris, the company performed at the Théâtre de la Ville, a very popular venue for modern dance. They were a huge hit, selling out all performances. People would parade outside the theater with signs offering to pay double for a ticket. After performances, I'd go out with Alvin to Café de Flor.

One evening, while I was at the theater, I met a young Moroccan man who looked to be in his early 20s named Abdul, and we became acquainted, meeting every now and then during the engagement. Alvin saw us together and told me he wanted to meet him. I introduced them, and Alvin quickly became very attached to him. I was out of the picture then, and only watched the two of them from a distance.

Back in New York, Alvin told me that he liked Abdul and wanted to help him in any way he could. Alvin asked for my help in getting his address and in getting him the papers he needed to come to the United States. I promised Alvin I would try, and in about a week I was able to find his name and address and arrange for his visit. Shortly after, the young man arrived, and I was very surprised by the speed with which this happened. Alvin again asked my help in finding Abdul a place to live, and I was able to get him a room at International House, north of Columbia University in Manhattan, where many foreign students stay.

We put him in there because it was very inexpensive, though Alvin paid all the bills in what was to become a big love affair in Alvin's life. The young man was rather uneducated and of a limited intelligence, but he was very good-looking. Naturally, he took advantage of Alvin, who was always taking him shopping and giving him money.

Since that vacation in Morocco, I had known that Alvin used drugs. He never discussed his addiction with me because he knew I was against it. (I have no patience whatsoever with anyone who abuses drugs.) Alvin liked to go to a seedy bar on Eighth Avenue after a performance, and if he asked me to join him, I'd watch him meet his entourage. I could see that this was the place where he got his supply. Alvin seemed drawn to a very low-class kind of people. I believe he enjoyed feeling a kind of control over them. But, in fact, all these people were always after their own favors—mostly, Alvin's money. That's why he was often in tight financial straits. Any time he had some money, he'd spend it immediately on drugs and on these people who were usually unemployed and in need of a bit of help. They found the right man: Alvin was a very good-hearted person, and he liked to help everybody. Unfortunately, this didn't add much to the quality of his life.

I used to go to the Ailey studio each morning, and one morning Alvin walked in and began to behave strangely. I could tell immediately that something was wrong—you could see it in his eyes. When he was in a bad mood, he could be extremely nasty to everybody, including me. Usually that mood meant he had picked up the wrong person, or things weren't working out with his current companion, or that person had taken all his money. That morning he said, "Paul, I want you to go to International House. I've been phoning him for days and no one answers. Go and find out where he is. He doesn't want to see me anymore and I cannot stand it. I have to see him."

I tried to explain to Alvin that, chances are, the young man was not really interested in him. He was only out for a good time or wanted to make some cash. But Alvin could never believe anything like that. I don't even think the young man was gay. I think he let himself get picked up for business. He was a hustler.

Following Alvin's orders, I went up to International House, found the manager, and learned that Abdul was still living there. I called Alvin and said, "He's here." A few more days passed, and when Alvin still had not heard from Abdul, Alvin, growing more and more frustrated, finally went to International House himself to find him. By the time he got there, he must have been completely out of control. As I was informed, he went upstairs and made an enormous uproar, banging on the door and shouting to be let into the young man's room. He tried to break down the door. But, in fact, by then Abdul was no longer at International House.

I got a telephone call from the management to come uptown immediately. When I got there, Alvin, completely out of his mind, was being restrained by security guards. I ran to the manager to explain who Alvin Ailey was, because no one at International House seemed to know, but the manager didn't care. Alvin continued fighting and screaming. Finally, the police were called, and when they arrived, Alvin became even more violent, so violent that he had to be handcuffed. Even with the handcuffs on, he still fought the policemen. He had such a twisted look on his face that he looked like a monster.

They wanted to take him to the police station. I called Stanley Plesent, then chairman of the Ailey board of directors, and he came immediately. Stanley, a lawyer, was able to give the police a guarantee, so that Alvin could be taken to Bellevue Hospital rather than to jail. He was placed in a huge dormitory, behind locked doors.

By this time, the press was alerted, and soon every newspaper carried the story of Alvin's having been taken into custody after going berserk at International House. At first, no one was permitted to see him. Later, Alvin sent a message saying that he would allow two or three people to visit. I was one of them. I rushed to the hospital and found him to be very calm. He stayed there for a while, and I saw him several times. Each time he wanted to know what had happened to Abdul.

Evidently, Abdul flew back to Europe while Alvin was in Bellevue. After Bellevue, Stanley arranged for Alvin to be admitted to an institution, where he stayed for a few months.

I felt awful about the whole situation, and guilty because I was the one who had brought the two of them together in the first place. Had I even imagined what the outcome would be, I never would have made that introduction.

While Alvin was confined, Ivy Clarke ran the company. Much later, a big shock came when Ivy was fired, without warning or cause, as far as I could determine. What made the dismissal worse is that it was done in such a terrible way. Many people do not realize how cruel a person Alvin could be. If you really knew him, you eventually became aware that this marvelously talented, extremely intelligent person had something mean within him that led him to do things that you would not expect from someone of his kindness and gifts. Alvin could never face reality. When he did bad things to other people, he did not want to be present. He would simply disappear.

In the case of Ivy Clarke, he was incapable of confronting her in person and had somebody else do his dirty work. She cleaned out her desk, packed up, and never saw him again. For years, she could not get over that he could do this to the one person who had kept the company together and thereby saved his life, who had looked after and comforted him throughout the hard times. She never forgave Alvin for the way he handled her firing. She would always tell me, "How could he do this to somebody who saved his life? You better be careful, Paul. You don't know Alvin. I do. It happened to me and it will happen to you. Just watch."

Another instance of his irresponsibility occurred when Alvin went to Israel to put on a ballet for the Bat-Dor Company. He called me every day from Tel Aviv, telling me how difficult it was for him to work there and how he wanted to come home. I said, "Alvin, you cannot do that because you've already been paid, and you've already spent that money, so you can't give it back even if you wanted to. You have to stay there until you are finished. Don't even mention coming home."

While we laughed about it, he'd still call me and say he wanted to return. He was miserable. One day I got a telephone call from the director of Bat-Dor. She said, "Mr. Szilard, we are sitting here in the studio and Alvin has not shown up for rehearsal. We are extremely nervous. He is not at the hotel. We've checked everywhere. We're afraid that something terrible has happened, and called the police. Mr. Szilard, do you have any idea what might have happened to Alvin?"

"I have no idea," I said.

I was very annoyed and afraid, because I imagined he went out the night before and got into some kind of trouble.

The next day I got a telephone call from Alvin.

"My God, Alvin," I said, "it sounds as if you're standing beside me. Where are you?"

"I'm in New York," he said.

"What? You are in New York?" I was flabbergasted.

"I just couldn't stand it anymore, so I took a plane back home."

He left Israel without saying a word to the Bat-Dor Company, who were not only waiting around for rehearsals but had become so concerned about his whereabouts.

Of course, the ballet was canceled.

I could not condone this kind of behavior, even though with me Alvin was always very fair. I was disappointed that a person of his gifts would treat people this way. Even in the office, when something difficult came up, he chose not to make a decision. On many occasions he was like an ostrich, sticking his head in the sand to avoid a situation. It always made me furious when he acted like this.

I think that there was more than one Alvin Ailey. Sometimes the irresponsible, destructive Alvin took over from the generous and loving creator.

I negotiated a contract for a ten-week tour of Australia with a major promoter there who was eager to bring the Ailey company over. The tour had to be of this length because the expenses involved in traveling such a great distance required substantial time for the promoter to recoup his investment. When we arrived in Australia, we debuted in a huge theater in Sydney. From the start

Alvin had the feeling that many Australians were racists. I did not share that feeling at first, but I came to agree with him. Our opening night in Sydney was a tremendous success with the public, but the next morning, the critic of the city's most important newspaper bad-mouthed the company in such a tasteless way that it was obvious how racist he was. *Revelations*, a hit everywhere it plays in the world, he reduced to nothing. How could he say that it is not a good ballet, or that it is not worthy, even if it wasn't to his personal taste? He wrote that the boys looked like waiters and the girls looked like Harlem prostitutes. He hated the costumes and everything else about the production. I was so enraged I sat down with the company manager and we immediately wrote an open letter to the editor of the newspaper, saying that on the basis of the review one could only assume that his critic was a racist. We further charged that what he wrote showed he knew nothing about dance. The next morning the letter was printed in the Sydney newspaper, to its credit. It had a huge impact on the dance scene in Australia, so much so that the director of the Australian Ballet called to congratulate me. It seemed everybody in Australia hated this critic, but no one had dared to openly admit it. Finally, somebody had said what so many people had felt for years.

Sophisticated Ladies

One day some Broadway producers came to my office because they needed a choreographer for their new show. "We must have Alvin Ailey," they said.

"I can tell you right off the bat that he hates doing Broadway shows."

"Why?" they asked. The reason was simple: Alvin was not a choreographer who could make a ballet on deadline. He had a mental block, and he always told me that he would never accept a Broadway assignment because he was afraid he wouldn't be ready in time for opening night.

But I pointed out that this show, which they were calling *So-*

phisticated Ladies, was different: it was all about the music of Duke Ellington, one of Alvin's heroes. Duke Ellington was to Alvin what Stravinsky was to Balanchine.

"This is fantastic, Alvin," I said. "I think you should do it."

"I'm not the kind of choreographer who can guarantee them that in four weeks I'll be finished. I need time. I want to be loose. When I want to be finished, then I'll be finished," Alvin said.

I was annoyed that Alvin turned it down. I thought it would have been a great opportunity for him, and would have provided him with some decent income.

At Alvin's insistence, I eventually had to tell the producers no. But I had a suggestion for leading lady: "Why don't you take Judith Jamison."

They thought it was an interesting idea, but were skeptical because Judi had never been in a Broadway show. The producers and I went back and forth on this. It seemed that on Broadway you have to have a big name, and though Judi was very well known in the dance world, she was not expected to be much of a draw for theatergoers.

"Don't worry," I said. "She is such a big name that people have heard of her even outside the world of dance."

"Well, if we take Judi Jamison, we must have a partner who is an established Broadway name."

"One thing at a time," I told them.

A few weeks later they came back and said, "Yes. We want Judi Jamison."

Once that was decided, I insisted on getting star billing for her—her name above the title. After some negotiations, they finally agreed to that, too.

"Well, who is going to be her partner?" They suggested various male dancers, all of whom Judi vetoed. It was beginning to seem like *Turandot*. Then suddenly Judi got very excited and announced that she knew the perfect person to be her partner—Gregory Hines.

The producers were not too happy with this suggestion. After all, Gregory too was relatively unknown at this time, aside from his appearances on the nightclub circuit dancing with his brother. But while the producers resisted, Judi insisted, finally telling them that she would not do the show unless Gregory was her partner. They had no choice. Soon after, I signed the contract for Judi, and Gregory Hines was hired.

Opening night was an overwhelming success for Judi and Gregory, who became instant Broadway stars. Eventually the relationship between them soured. I believe Judi, sensing he was upstaging her, felt more and more frustrated. And as the situation got worse, Judi began to hate the show and wanted no more part of it. "Take me out of it," she said, but that was impossible.

During the winter, when a performance was over, Judi would bundle herself up in sweaters and a hat, and, looking nothing like the star of a Broadway show, she would quickly escape from the theater through the back door to the parking lot where she left her car.

"Judi," I said, "why don't you go out the stage door and sign some autographs. There are people waiting to see you."

"No. I won't do it," she said.

Gregory Hines, on the other hand, still dripping after a performance, would stand in the freezing cold and give autographs to whoever asked for one.

Nevertheless, Gregory left the show before Judi did, and his brother, Maurice Hines, took over his role. He and Judi got along famously.

When her contract expired after two years, the producers asked her to perform in London, Japan, and throughout Europe, but Judi refused.

Pas de Duke (Jamison and Baryshnikov)

Alvin and I were talking about an upcoming gala at City Center, trying to figure out what he should present. We always fed each other ideas. Sometimes he accepted what I said, at other times he did not. But for this occasion I came up with a wonderful idea: How about Baryshnikov and Judi together?

Alvin thought that was brilliant and immediately got excited by the idea. He chose music by Duke Ellington and named the *pas de deux* he choreographed *Pas de Duke*. After Baryshnikov and I settled on terms, rehearsals began. Rouben Ter-Arutunian designed the wonderful set and costumes. When I looked in at rehearsals, I thought Misha was very good, but he was no Alvin Ailey dancer. Judi, on the other hand, slender and gorgeous and looking like a million dollars, was sensational. They danced beautifully together, but I felt that Judi was tops. She was so jazzy, and so filled with the vocabulary of Alvin Ailey, that nobody else could have danced it the way she did. Because Misha was a little bit handicapped by being a classical dancer who had never worked with Alvin before, Alvin had to tailor the choreography to fit Misha's talents. Alvin devised a lot of balletic moves that looked good on Misha, and Misha brought them off, knowing he had a formidable partner and giving his all.

The two of them created quite a fire on stage, as each tried to outdo the other.

Patrick Dupond

Patrick Dupond is a superstar of France, an *étoile* (the top rank of dancer in the Paris Opera Ballet) who has been decorated repeatedly for his brilliant dancing. In France, he's received like a rock star, and when he dances, thousands of people show up. As a young dancer, seventeen or eighteen years old, he performed at the ballet competition in Varna, Bulgaria, and won first prize. He still is an unbelievable dancer, not just a strong technician but a true artist as well.

Patrick has such a strong personality and emanates such sweetness that he holds the audience from the time he first appears on stage until he exits. Your eyes go right to him, and he has the talent of a wonderful actor that makes him appear to be dancing for you alone. The only problem with him is that he's lazy; he knows he has a natural technique and feels he doesn't have to work very hard.

When I discovered Patrick, he was only eighteen years old but already appearing with the Paris Opera Ballet. The first time I saw him dance there as a *sujet* (soloist), I said to myself, "This boy is going to become a sensation, and I am going to do what I can to make it happen." I dashed off to the Opera House and spoke first to prima ballerina Noëlla Pontois, their reigning star, in her dressing room. "Darling," I said, "I would like you to meet with Patrick Dupond."

"Who???" she asked.

"You don't know who Patrick Dupond is?" I said.

"No." She didn't have a clue.

It took me two days to find Patrick because nobody knew anything about him. When I did finally locate him I told him that I wanted to bring him to America, to the Chicago Opera House, for which I would soon be arranging a gala.

He was in heaven.

When I returned to the United States I went as usual to Mrs. Geraldine Freund, the art patron in Chicago. Again she wanted her next gala to be an extraordinary event and she had asked me to bring somebody special from Europe. Now I told her that I would bring over Patrick Dupond.

Patrick was so young at the time he was not permitted to sign the contract. Max Bozzoni, then and now his teacher at the Paris Opera, signed it for him. Bozzoni, my classmate when I studied dance at the Studio Wacker in Paris, had been a star of the Paris Opera before becoming ballet master.

When I brought Patrick to Chicago for his American debut, he was an immediate sensation. The house was sold out and his performance was greeted with a thunderous ovation. After that, I brought him to New York, to dance with the American Ballet Theatre at the Metropolitan Opera House. Makarova wanted to feature him in her production of *Bayadère*, and I worked out the contract with Lucia Chase.

In all, I arranged for Patrick to dance at four different Chicago galas for Mrs. Freund. With so many stars involved there were naturally backstage intrigues and jealousies. On one of these programs, Baryshnikov also danced. I felt that Misha never appreciated Patrick, who was very young, very beautiful, and afforded Misha enormous competition.

When any of my dancers performed, I often watched from the wings. You never know what can happen. Injuries can occur in a split second. Once, when I was in the wings watching Patrick, I could see Misha coming towards me, still applying his makeup as he walked. Apparently, he didn't want to miss Patrick's performance, which brought the audience to their feet, applauding and shouting. So everyone was impressed except for Misha. He just said, "Bah. Awful," and turned back toward his dressing room.

On the way out, I met Misha's agent, and said, "Wasn't Patrick fantastic? And you know, he's only eighteen years old."

"Now look, Paul," he said, "how much longer is he going to be eighteen years old?"

"Until he's nineteen," I said. I didn't miss a beat.

One day, I approached Georges Hirsch, director of the Paris Opera Ballet, and asked him to invite Alvin Ailey to do a new ballet for the Paris Opera. As his father was a former director of that company, I have known Georges since he was a child. He thought it was a wonderful idea, and so did Alvin, who got to work immediately on a ballet he would call *Au Bord du Précipice*. The work was suggested by the life of the hard-living rock star, Jim Morrison of the Doors, who died in Paris in 1970. It would be Alvin's first time as a choreographer at the Paris Opera Ballet. He and I arrived in Paris together, and he began to cast the ballet. He chose three casts. The first starred Patrick Dupond, with Monique Loudières; the second, Charles Jude, a French-Vietnamese dancer; and the third, Michaël Denard. In my opinion Denard was completely wrong for the character based on Jim Morrison, and his casting surprised me. But in fact, sometimes Alvin would work that way, challenging a dancer and giving him or her something to work against. And although Denard, purely classical, didn't have much feeling for Alvin's modern technique, Alvin liked him anyway.

We started rehearsals with a large cast. They were very exciting, and we all could see that *Au Bord du Précipice* was going to be something special. It was very interesting and very imaginative; I believe Alvin was extremely inspired by Patrick Dupond and his overwhelming personality.

The Paris Opera Ballet's directors told me they never had had a choreographer like Alvin, whom the dancers were willing to follow blindly. If he wanted to work ten hours, the dancers worked ten hours. If Alvin wanted to work on Sundays, the dancers would show up on Sundays. They did not care about union rules and regulations. They responded to Alvin's charisma and they loved him. He became a guru to dancers he had just met. It was like a chemical reaction. His enthusiasm was infectious.

A young dancer of mixed blood from the French colonies, Eric Vu An, caught Alvin's eye. He was a handsome young man no more than eighteen years old. Alvin was interested in him, not only because he was so good-looking, but because he was a wonderful dancer as well.

The ballet was of course constructed around the character based on Jim Morrison, to be danced first by Patrick. At the end, while Patrick lay dying, Eric was making a show of technical bravura around him. Naturally, Patrick, there on the floor, got furious at what was going on. During a break, he came to me, exasperated.

"What is Alvin doing?" he said, "Does he think I am going to kill myself for this ballet, and that kid—not even a principal dancer—is going to close the curtain and upstage me? Absolutely not. It is out of the question, and I will not agree to that."

This crisis caused an uproar among the whole company. Alvin didn't know how to handle the situation. I went up to him and said, "Patrick is right. He's the star of the evening. You cannot close the curtain with the star doing nothing on the floor, while another dancer, though very good, takes all the applause."

Many of the Paris Opera dancers wanted Vu An out because he was not a principal dancer. In the large European opera houses, there are rules and regulations concerning which dancers are eligible for which roles. One afternoon, Vu An handed me a letter to give to Alvin. In it, he asked Alvin not to listen to the people who were jealous of him, accusing them of being racists. That charge profoundly upset Alvin, and he refused to take Vu An out of the ballet.

"Absolutely not," Alvin said. "He stays in. I will do what I want."

But Alvin still didn't know what to do. Typically for him, he had promised the role to Vu An. (He promised everything to everybody). But Alvin also had to keep Patrick happy; after all, he danced the lead and Alvin respected him as an artist. Finally, he changed the ending of the ballet, pleasing Patrick by keeping the focus on his character.

Paris Opera spent a fortune on the ballet, and it proved to be a great success. A few years later the Ailey company was invited to perform at the Metropolitan Opera for a two-week engagement. This was a very big opportunity, because no company like Alvin's had ever played the Met before. Alvin wanted to do something exceptional, and I suggested that we do *Au Bord du Précipice*, with Patrick and Loudières as guest artists. Alvin thought it was a fabulous idea, and I immediately got on the phone to the Paris Opera to negotiate for the rights to perform the ballet.

Naturally, the Ailey company could not afford to have new sets and costumes made. I succeeded in getting the Paris Opera Ballet to lend us, at absolutely no cost, their scenery and costumes, with everything to be flown over from France. The signed contract stated that after the two-week engagement at the Met, whatever we had borrowed had to be shipped back immediately to the Paris Opera in proper condition.

Months later I got a letter from the Paris Opera wanting to know what had happened to the costumes and scenery. Nothing had been returned to them. Furious, I went to Bill Hammond, who was general manager at the time, and asked for an explanation.

"Oh, well, it was so marvelous, I decided to take it on the road."

"Bill," I said, "you only had permission to perform it at the Met. How dare you do this?"

"Well, I took it anyhow and will send it back to them after," he said.

So, when the U.S. tour (in which I played no part) was over, he returned the scenery and the costumes. Not only were they six months late, but everything was in terrible condition. The costumes hadn't even been cleaned, and the shoes, made of very expensive suede, were torn to shreds. The Paris Opera was of course enraged.

Alvin, a man born for the theater, knew exactly what to do on stage. Even when his choreography was not his strongest, it always looked good because Alvin knew exactly how to stage it.

Many times, Alvin told me that he needed a rest and wanted to take a year off and do nothing. He even mentioned closing the company and living in Paris for a year, but that would have affected the lives of too many people. Of course, it never happened.

Wherever I book the company, the ballet that everyone wants to see is *Revelations*, which I call the *Swan Lake* of the Ailey Dance Theater. But one day Alvin got so sick and tired of *Revelations* that he decided to remove the ballet from the program. "I do not want to do *Revelations* anymore. We are going to do without it for a while," he said.

"Impossible," I told him, "I've already booked the company, and *Revelations* has been promised."

He didn't care. He just stormed out of the room.

I called him later in his office and said, "Alvin, you cannot do this. Everybody expects *Revelations*, and I have the signed contracts. If you do not do it, I will cancel the European tour." And I slammed down the phone.

He called me back and said in his gruffest voice, "All right, you can put it in, but you'll see how unpleasant I will be."

Deep down he knew he could not take away *Revelations*. It was the mainstay of his repertory. I think he just wanted a change.

❀ ❀ ❀

The great force of the Alvin Ailey company lies with its dancers, because they are accessible human beings in performance. They bring to the stage a certain element that immediately endears them to spectators. In classical ballet, almost always you feel a certain distance between the dancers onstage and the public. Not with Alvin Ailey. The company is bursting with exciting, sexy, and gorgeous-looking people who have astonishing emotional impact. They take the audience by the hand, as it were, the minute the curtain rises, and never let go. Even if the ballet is unknown, it is immediately accepted by the audience on account of the personalities of the dancers and the way they perform. This unique connection between the public and the artists is why I love the company. I consider myself to be a member of the Ailey family. And most members of the audience feel the same way.

That is the secret of the Ailey success. I'm lucky to have this company to book, because it is wanted everywhere in the world—Israel, Italy, Greece, Denmark, and most recently South Africa, to name just a few.

The Ailey company enjoyed tremendous success in Copenhagen. There a young fellow came to the ballet with amazing frequency. In fact, each time we played, he appeared. He became a good friend of Alvin's, which was normal, because Alvin enjoyed the company of young people. Finally, however, I figured out that this was not just a friendship—the young man was supplying Alvin with dope. I said nothing to Alvin, but one day I called this boy aside and said, "I know why you are here all the time and I know why you are after Alvin. I don't like it, and I don't want you to show up any more. Please just disappear, and don't come back."

I felt that I had done my duty.

The directors of the Royal Danish Opera House were intent on having a new ballet from Alvin. He set *The River* for them and it was performed brilliantly. The Danish company included a marvelous but no-longer-young leading dancer, Mette. Because of her age, she was usually given little to do, but Alvin liked her very much and decided that he was going to make a solo for her.

While the company was rehearsing in Copenhagen, I had to go to Paris, where one day I got a phone call from one of the directors of the Royal Danish Ballet. He said, "Please, Mr. Szilard, we are having a problem. I can't explain it over the phone but you must come immediately." I was terrified but I could only guess. I took the first plane to Copenhagen, rushed to the Opera House and, out of breath, walked right up to the director.

"What has happened to Alvin?"

"We really don't know," he said, "But he acts so strange and so odd that we can't control him. Sometimes he's angry, sometimes he doesn't come in, and sometimes he talks gibberish."

I went straight to the hotel and in the elevator going up to Alvin's room I tried to imagine what might have happened. I thought maybe Alvin had acted offensively because he did not like the company or the dancers. That often happened when Alvin lost his patience with those he depended upon.

Alvin greeted me at the door looking fine. His manner was calm and his mood seemed pleasant.

"Come on," he said, "I have to get to the theater for rehearsal."

We hurried from the hotel to the stage door, and as we walked in, a young dancer came out and greeted Alvin with a friendly hello.

"Look," Alvin said sharply, "I don't like what you are doing. I don't like the way you dance, and I will not allow you to dance *Don Quixote*."

The dancer was of course very annoyed and upset, and I thought: How dare Alvin speak to a dancer like that in a company and about a ballet that are not his own. What was it his business if this dancer did well or not in *Don Q*?

As the dancer walked away, visibly shaken, I asked Alvin what was going on.

"Well, you'll never believe it," he said. "They've asked me to become artistic director of the Royal Opera House. And as artistic director, I don't like the way he dances, and I will not let him do it."

I realized at once that Alvin was talking nonsense. Why would they ask Alvin to head a ballet company? Something was wrong. We went upstairs and there he started behaving strangely. I knew immediately he must have been on dope and that the drugs were influencing his behavior. I had a meeting with the unnerved director, and told him that I, too, felt that something was not quite right with Alvin.

A few days later, Alvin told me to come to his hotel room to see something. When I arrived, he showed me five fur coats he had just bought at the most expensive furrier in Copenhagen, and had paid for with his credit card. Most of them were awful looking, because Alvin didn't have very good taste. The worst of the bunch was a fox cape which he gallantly swept off the bed and draped over my shoulders. "Why did you buy all these, Alvin?" I asked.

"I loved them. Why shouldn't I have them?" he shot back. "And this one," he said, "I have bought for you."

I almost died, because when he put it on me, I could see that the cape was made up of the bodies of the foxes, and their heads, about a dozen of them, were at my neck. I was hysterical inside but I dared not open my mouth because I could sense Alvin was already in a terrible mood.

"Oh, thank you, thank you," I said, trying to be as gracious as possible. But the minute I went back to my own room, I took it off and hung it in the closet. The back of the closet.

About two days later, Alvin knocked at my door, and when I opened it, there he stood in his pajamas.

"Where is the fur cape I gave you?" he demanded.

"It's over there," I said and pointed toward the closet.

"Give it to me," he said, "I know you hate it."

And he stormed out of the room, with the fox cape slung over his arm.

I was thrilled that he took it back!

We stayed at the most elegant hotel in Copenhagen. Very old-fashioned, filled with very distinguished, older people who dressed to the nines, even for breakfast. One day, the manager called me in my room, and said, "Please Mr. Szilard, can you do something about Mr. Ailey? He came down this morning to breakfast in his pajamas, and in his bare feet. We didn't know what to do. The other people in the dining room were shocked."

They wanted me to convince Alvin to eat in his room. I couldn't do that because the drugs were stronger than I was.

Then came the opening night of *The River*. The air was filled with excitement because Alvin was very popular in Copenhagen and the performance was sold out. The evening opened with the new solo number for the aging ballerina. I had seen Mette dance it in rehearsal and knew she was marvelous in the role. Even though she was not young, she had such artistic power her performance was magnificent. I had told Alvin at the time that what he had done for Mette was tremendous. Now together Alvin and I were backstage waiting for the performance to begin. Mette came on stage in costume and waited for the curtain to be raised. Suddenly Alvin went up to her and told her, "You are absolutely awful. I don't like the way you are dancing. I should never have let you do it." Then he walked away. Mette was in shock, started crying, and yelled, "After this, I don't want to dance."

With Alvin gone, I ran up to her and tried to comfort her. "Don't pay attention to what he says. He is sick. Can't you see that he is sick? Don't take it seriously. You are marvelous and will have a tremendous success with this ballet."

"No," she said, "I can't go out after this."

"Please, believe me," I said. "He doesn't mean a word of it. He wouldn't have done it for you if he didn't feel that you were wonderful from the beginning."

Finally, Mette regained her composure, the curtain rose, and she went on to achieve a triumph. Maybe all the stress was good for her, because she had gotten so worked up that her performance emotions were at their peak.

After the performance, however, she was still distraught, and so I invited her, along with other dancers, to have a drink at the hotel bar. Then I went to the house phone and called Alvin in his room.

"Alvin, how are you?" I asked.

"I'm OK. How was it?"

"An enormous success. Why did you leave?"

"I couldn't stand it anymore. How was she?"

"She was fantastic. Alvin, please do me a favor. She was so shocked by what you said to her before she went on that I think you should come downstairs and have a drink with us."

"No, I don't want to do that."

"Alvin, please."

"Oh, OK. I'll see." And he hung up the phone.

In five minutes he came down to the bar, in casual clothes, but barefoot. He went to the bar and ordered a drink. When he came to our table he spoke directly to Mette. "Listen," he said, "I want to talk to you. Come up to my room."

They went upstairs together.

Twenty minutes later she came back into the bar, with a fur cape draped around her shoulders. Not the one he gave to me and took back. This one was even more awful than that.

"Imagine," she said, "He gave this to me because he heard how fantastic I was in the ballet." He also had told her how wonderful a dancer she was. She was in heaven. Everything was now fabulous, and Alvin's backstage performance had been forgotten.

Unlike me, she got to keep her cape!

Alvin was slowly going downhill. He would disappear in the morning and it would take hours to find him. Sometimes he just didn't want to talk to me, and at other times he was extremely rude. I tried my best to be with him as often as possible. The Royal Danish Opera did not know what to do, since they felt that Alvin might do something dangerous and put the lives of the dancers in jeopardy.

Interestingly enough, while all of this was going on, I got a phone call at four in the morning from Alvin's mother, Lula Cooper, who lived in Los Angeles. She had a sixth sense when it came to her son, and now she felt in her heart that something was wrong. Lula was a very tough lady. No nonsense.

"Paul," she said, "what's wrong with my son?"

"What do you mean, Lula?" I knew what was wrong, but did not wish to worry her.

"I feel it. There is something going on. You tell me."

"Lula, I have nothing to tell you. Alvin's new ballet was an enormous success. Everything went very well."

"Don't lie to me, Paul" she said, "I know that you are lying to me. If you don't tell me the truth, I am getting on the plane and I will see you tomorrow morning."

"Lula, it is four o'clock in the morning, and I am not going to disturb Alvin. If you want, I will have him call you tomorrow."

"No, Paul, that is not good enough. If you don't tell me the truth then I will be there tomorrow morning."

"You do what you want, Lula, but there is no use in your coming," I said once again, but she wasn't buying it. We hung up, and in the morning, I went to Alvin to tell him that his mother had called.

"Tell her not to come," Alvin said, "I do not want to see her. I will immediately go away. I will take a plane in the other direction if I know she's coming here."

Alvin, who had not slept in his room, disappeared for a while that night, and when I finally found him, he was in a very bad state. I was too afraid of his rages to ask him too many details. Unable to control the situation any further, I felt I needed the involvement of the Ailey company.

I called Bill Hammond, executive director of the company, in New York, and told him to come to Copenhagen immediately because Alvin was in a terrible condition. Bill took the first available plane over. Carol Vollet Garner, the talented Ailey costumer, was with me in Copenhagen, and when Bill arrived, we filled him in on the situation. It was agreed that while I remained in Europe, Bill would accompany Alvin back home. At that point, however, Alvin disappeared again. It was night, and we could not find him anywhere.

An old friend of Alvin's, a former dancer who had lived in Copenhagen, told us there was a hotel near the sea where he thought Alvin might be with a young fellow he was seeing. I suspected that this was the young man who had been supplying Alvin with drugs. Late at night Bill and I took a car and drove for hours, not knowing where we were. Finally, we reached the sea and came upon the hotel, looking ghostly in the moonlight. When we walked inside, I went up to the desk of the night clerk and asked, "Is Mr. Ailey here?"

"Yes," he said.

We had found him.

I called Alvin up in his room, and when he answered, I said, "Alvin, it's me, Paul."

"What are you doing here?" he demanded to know.

"We came to see you because we could not find you anywhere. Are you OK?"

He was furious.

"How dare you come looking for me? How dare you come and follow me? It's my own private business."

"Alvin, it's no longer your private business. I am here with Bill . . ."

"Bill," he shouted, "what is he doing here?"

"He had business here. Alvin, please calm down. Come downstairs. We have to talk."

Surprisingly, Alvin didn't fight us on this, and he came downstairs. Bill and I tried to explain that something was wrong with him and he needed help. We told him that he needed to go home. He came back with us to the hotel in Copenhagen, where we made arrangements for him to fly back to the United States with Bill.

When I returned to New York, while it was very obvious that something was seriously wrong with Alvin, nobody would say what it was. We all felt it and knew it, but nobody spoke of it.

Before Copenhagen, on tour in the south of France, we had been in Cannes, and many evenings Alvin and I had dinner together.

One evening we went out for fish, and after we ate, when we usually took a walk on the beach, he said, "I don't feel very well. I want to go back to the hotel."

"What's wrong? Did you take your pills?" I asked. I never asked him what the pills were for. I knew he was manic-depressive and taking pills for that, but I didn't know how many other medications he had with him.

"I'm not taking any," Alvin answered.

"Alvin, we are going back to the hotel and you are going to take your pills."

When we got to his room, I asked him where the pills were.

"You want to know where the pills are? Come with me and I will show you."

So he led me into the bathroom and pointed to the toilet. "That's where they are, Paul." He had taken all his medications, several thousand dollars worth, and flushed them down the toilet.

I looked at him in amazement.

"Paul, I am sick and tired of those pills and I will not swallow another."

Later on, catastrophe struck after we had all returned from Copenhagen. Alvin called me one morning, as he did each day, and in an alarmingly weak voice, he said, "Paul, you've got to help me. I feel awful. Please . . ."

"Of course, Alvin. Anything," I said.

"Get me a doctor," he begged.

"Alvin, you have a doctor."

"He's gone out of town." It was Saturday.

So I called my doctor, Dr. Albert Knapp, and told him about Alvin, whom he had never met. When I said that Alvin was sounding worse than ever before, he instructed me to bring Alvin to Lenox Hill Hospital, where Dr. Knapp was on the staff. The doctor made all the arrangements while I picked up Alvin in a taxi. At the time, he was living on Eighth Avenue, in the 50s, and he still wouldn't let me into his apartment. I can only imagine what it must have looked like. That morning as soon as I saw Alvin, I thought this was the end. He could barely walk, and looked as if he was living on borrowed time.

When we arrived at the hospital, Dr. Knapp was already there waiting for him. I waited outside Alvin's room while he was being examined. About ten minutes later Dr. Knapp came out and told me that if I had brought him in two or three days later, it would have been too late. The doctor didn't tell me what he had, but I could guess. He remained at the hospital for a few weeks. I visited him every day, and watched Alvin's condition get progressively worse. By this time, it was obvious what he had, but no one would talk about it. AIDS was not spoken of as easily as it is today, more than ten years later. But those closest to Alvin knew the truth.

Each time I saw him he begged me to bring him some split pea soup. I bought two thermoses, so that I could deliver a fresh container of soup each time I saw him. We would talk about the company and about future plans. He never really gave me the feeling that he knew he was dying, that he had a disease that could not be cured. Indeed, we never discussed his illness. I would sit and talk with him for hours, and he expressed his annoyance about many things, mainly that his own company had never paid him proper royalties for his choreography, and had never compensated him for the ballets he had set for them. He drew a salary, of course, but nothing more. He also complained that the company was not making enough money, and bitterly criticized some people in the organization that he no longer liked. One day, he just burst out, "I cannot stand Bill Hammond. I want to fire him."

"Alvin, are you out of your mind? How can you fire the executive director of the company when you are in the hospital? How is the company going to run? You cannot do that."

"No. I want to fire him," he insisted.

Of course, Alvin had no real reason to fire Bill. It was part of his delirium. I begged him not to go through with it now, but to put it off until he got back to the office. Finally, Alvin agreed to wait until then to make a decision.

One day I said to Alvin, "You do not have a will. Everybody

must have a will. It does not mean you are dying. Even I have a will."

"I don't need a will. I have nothing," Alvin said. He was becoming agitated.

"That's not true," I said, trying to calm him down.

"I don't know how to make a will."

"Well, I'll arrange it for you."

I called Theodore Vittoria, my lawyer, who then went to the hospital to draft Alvin's will, along with one of his partners to act as witness. I was sitting with Alvin at the time, but I left the room in order to give them their privacy. I never asked what was in Alvin's will. I only know that he called the lawyer a couple of times because he kept changing his mind, and that Vittoria returned to the hospital on more than one occasion.

The days that followed were awful, until one day Alvin seemed better, and shortly after was sent home. The improvement didn't last very long, and soon he had to go back to the hospital—for the last time. He never came out. Near the end he told me, "Paul, I have the feeling that I'm never going to leave this hospital." I replied, "Don't be silly. You will walk out in no time."

"No, Paul," Alvin said, "This time I am sure. I'm glad you told me to make a will because I want to make sure that my mother has been taken care of."

He also said he didn't know what to do with the company. He didn't know whether to close it or to continue.

"Why should you close? It's your company. It's a marvelous company . . ." I said.

He sat up in bed.

"But, Paul, who should take over the company?"

Alvin had promised the company to so many people over the years. He promised it to Ulysses Dove. He promised it to George Faison. He promised it to several other dancer/choreographers who had been in the company. It was just like Alvin to promise the moon to everyone. I said, "In my opinion, the only one who should have it is the one who worked with you the longest and in the most important period of your life: Judi Jamison."

I felt that only Judi had the artistic integrity to be director of the company. Also, while the other choices were fine dancers and choreographers, only Judi had that diva attitude which always impresses the public and conveys leadership. I felt that people would want to support Judi and be on her side.

He thought it over for a second and said, "Well . . . let me think about it."

Later on, I found out that the board and Judi agreed that Judi should take over as Artistic Director of the company.

And then Alvin got worse week by week, day by day. Soon there came a time when I was told that it was useless for me to go to the hospital, but I kept going. He would just lie in bed without opening his mouth. I didn't know if he was conscious or not. When I gave him my hand, he held onto it and squeezed it every once in a while. I don't even know if he knew whether it was me or not.

One day, after sitting by his side for a while, I bent over and asked him how he was doing. "Alvin, how are you?" I said.

He looked back at me with eyes that looked like glass. They showed no emotion. In those last weeks, his mother, some friends and dancers came to see him. I know that Judi was there along with Sylvia Waters and Mrs. Cooper and Stanley Plesent, among others.

When the doctor told me that he could go at any minute. I went into his room and once again took Alvin's hand. "Alvin, do you know who I am? It's Paul." He looked at me through glazed eyes. It was as if he were already dead. He said nothing, but was able to squeeze my hand a little. There was something in his eyes, and in the touch of his hand, that told me he knew who I was, even though he couldn't speak anymore. The tears began to roll down my face, and I left the room.

A few minutes later, Alvin was gone.

Alvin's funeral was at the Cathedral of St. John the Divine, in Manhattan. Over six thousand people came to pay their respects to Alvin. The service was broadcast to overflow crowds on the streets outside. Inside, we had to line up and walk in a procession.

It was all choreographed. Among the speakers were Maya Angelou, Judith Jamison, Carmen de Lavallade, and myself. When it was my turn, I had to climb the stairs to the pulpit, and like the captain of a ship, looked out onto a sea of people.

"Alvin," I said when I was ending my speech, "I have to say adieu to you because we are going to different places. You are definitely going up there, but I am definitely going down there. I don't think we'll meet." Needless to say, everyone laughed, except the clergy in the front row.

A few weeks later, Alvin's will was read. Sylvia Waters was named executor of the estate, along with Alvin's bank. The reading disclosed that most people in Alvin's circle got something. Alvin's mother Lula inherited all his money, most of his possessions, and the rights to Alvin's ballets.

I expected some kind of remembrance and was shocked when my name was not mentioned. Alvin did not leave me so much as a photo or an ashtray. The biggest surprise was that Alvin left Bill Hammond his collection of Haitian paintings, even though Alvin would have fired him had I not intervened on Bill's behalf.

I could not get over it for days—to be overlooked after being such a close friend. I openly showed my disappointment and told people I was hurt. And then I remembered Ivy's warning to me about Alvin's character, and it looked as if her prediction had come true.

Even to this day, I cannot figure out why he did this. When I try to analyze it, I come up with nothing definite. Sometimes I feel that he was jealous of me. Maybe he felt I shouldn't have charged the company for my services, because he and I had become as close as brothers. Or was there another reason for his not remembering me in his will?

For a time, I thought I would stop booking the company. Sylvia and Lula came to me when they heard this and said that I'd be out of my mind to do something like that. Then they called me one day to say they were going to give me two paintings from Alvin's estate.

"Please don't dare send anything to me, because if you do, I am throwing it right out," I said.

Despite my protests, they sent me the two paintings. I immediately called a friend of mine in Washington who had been a dancer and I asked him if he wanted two paintings that had belonged to Alvin Ailey. He said yes, and I arranged for him to pick them up the next time he came to New York.

Of course, I loved Alvin, and I finally came to understand that he was a sick man and that I'd never know the reasons for his actions. But for a long time it hurt.

Alvin hated society types. He liked his own crowd, liked hanging out in bars and cheap dives with his own friends. He didn't like to dress up and go to parties. I suffered from having to lie and make up excuses for Alvin's behavior, because he never liked to do what was necessary for a man in his position. I was always begging him to appear here and there for fundraisers, but though he wanted to get the money, he never wanted to socialize to raise funds.

Alvin was one of my best friends, and I would have done anything for him. When I was with Alvin it was a twenty-four hour a day job. I know that he loved me.

Judith Jamison

1999 was a very interesting year in many ways. The most outstanding event for me came in November, when Judith Jamison was decorated at the Kennedy Center in Washington, D.C. for her "Lifetime Achievement in the Performing Arts." It made me very proud to be there in the audience to watch Judi receive her award, just as I had been there for Alvin when he won his, about ten years before, under President Reagan. Invitations to the White House are extremely limited but Judi had said I deserved to be with her for that occasion. The evening was hosted by President and Mrs. Clinton, and Judi was decorated alongside Jason Robards, Victor Borge, Sean Connery, and Stevie Wonder. Judi, diva that she is, was the queen of the evening.

There is something about Judi that commands your attention

immediately, no matter who else is onstage. In 1971, Alvin choreographed *Cry* as a gift for his mother, and Judi, dancing the lead,
became a star. *Life* magazine published a series of photos of her
performing in *Cry*, and the reaction to that publicity was extraordinary. From then on, Judi became more and more important to
the company. In Paris, the public treated her like a new Josephine
Baker. She was the toast of the town, but she was always very
down-to-earth and never let adulation go to her head.

One of my first engagements for the Ailey company was at the
Sadler's Wells Theatre in London. I negotiated quite a good guarantee, much more than they had seen up to that time. After I
made the contract, I was told by Alvin that Judi was not coming.
"What are you talking about?" I asked, "She has to come. She's
the star of the company."

"Well, Paul, she says she's not coming. I think you better go
and speak to her."

I found her at the theater and asked if what Alvin had told me
was correct. And it was.

"I'm not going because they are not paying me properly," she
answered.

I went back to Alvin to see what we could work out, because I
felt it was imperative that we have her.

"Alvin, what do you want me to do?" I asked.

"Paul," he said, "The company is almost broke. I can't pay her
more. If she doesn't want to go for the money we offered, then she
should stay home."

"No, I cannot accept that." I was very annoyed because Judi
was now a major star, and I had promised the Sadler's Wells management she would be there.

I came up with a solution: I would pay the difference. When
she named her price, I, thinking it was not all that unreasonable,
agreed to it, and she came to London with the rest of us. Judi only
asked one thing of me: not to give her the extra money in the theater. I agreed to give it to her separately. This was the plan: Across
the street from the Sadler's Wells Theatre was a coffee house
where all the artists would go after a performance. Judi's former

husband, Miguel, who was in London, spent time with the company in the coffee house. Judi didn't want him to know that she was getting extra money. We arranged that when payday arrived, we would be at the coffee house at a certain time. I'd give her a signal, we'd both go to the bathroom, and there, in the toilet, I'd hand Judi her extra money—and we would both burst into laughter. It happened every week until we left London.

Once Judi was acknowledged to be the most outstanding personality in the company, I became her personal agent and negotiated bookings for her all over the world. Each time she performed, usually dancing *Cry*, she was recognized as the astonishing star that she was and one of the most important dancers ever—a true diva. Of course she made a lot of money dancing in some of the most venerable theaters of the world: the Munich Opera, the Berlin Opera, the Vienna Opera.

John Neumeier, the American choreographer who is now director of the Hamburg Ballet, decided to make a ballet for her for the Vienna Opera. That became *Josephslegende* ("The Legend of Joseph"), which had originally been done for Diaghilev. Judi danced the role of Potiphar's wife and Kevin Hagen played the young slave with whom she falls in love. In the Diaghilev company, that part was originally danced by Léonide Massine when he was a young man.

Josephslegende took quite a long time to complete and several times Judi had to go to Europe to learn and practice her part. But it was all worth it, because opening night in Vienna was a sensation. The audience would not let her leave the stage. Applause and ovations lasted for at least ten minutes. I heard that none of the leading dancers in the company would agree to be Judi's understudy because of her enormous success. So for that reason, with no one else willing to dance her role, she was constantly returning to Europe. In Vienna she was treated like royalty. She had an exquisite dressing room, very close to the stage. Outside her door sat three women in white coats like nurses: a hairdresser, a stylist, and a dresser. When she was about to go onstage, they all followed her into the wings like ducklings. Her dressing room was filled with flowers and presents.

Judi has such a sense of artistic integrity that even her smallest movement can tell a story. There is one moment in the ballet when she reaches out to Joseph, wanting to touch him, but hesitates and withdraws her hand. I felt that the emotion of the entire ballet was conveyed in that one gesture. It explained the whole story of the ballet, and illustrated the tragedy: a queen may not fall in love with a slave. Judi was able to convey all that, and more, in the way she moved her arm and hand. Electricity came out of her, as she brought her every emotion to her fingertips.

Everything Judi did had artistic merit, meaning, and taste. Even now when she's no longer dancing, she is one of the biggest stars of the dance world. For me, there are only four dancers I consider the greatest of our time, and who excited me artistically: Anthony Dowell of the Royal Ballet, Natasha Makarova, Misha Baryshnikov, and Judi Jamison.

During the height of her popularity, Judi became one of the highest paid artists in the dance world. But she was also extravagant with her money. One day she said, "Come with me. I just ordered a silver fox coat." Off we went to the best furrier in Vienna to pick up the coat that had been made for her. It extended from her neck to the floor and she looked divine in it. Nobody can wear clothes like Judi.

Of course, Judi and I became close personal friends long ago. When she danced, she couldn't wait for me to come backstage to tell her what I thought about her performance. Today, I can't do the same thing with Miss Judith Jamison the artistic director. She listens to me, but in the end she does whatever she feels she has to do in her own way. It's more difficult to bring her around to my beliefs now that she's head of the Alvin Ailey Dance Theater.

Maurice Béjart is one of the most respected choreographers in Europe. His ballets are thoughtfully reviewed and admired all over the world. I feel that while Béjart is a good choreographer, he is more a master at theatricality. Since our days at Studio

Wacker in Paris, I've known him to be an extremely intelligent person. He looks electric, with his piercing blue eyes. We were both in Madame Rousanne's class, but he did not have the ideal body for a classical ballet dancer and was more of a character dancer. He was always drawn to choreographing. It's unfortunate that he has never been accepted by Anna Kisselgoff, the chief dance critic of the *New York Times*, who has reviewed his work harshly each time she has seen his company perform. The public, however, loves Béjart, even in New York.

Béjart adored Judi Jamison, considering her one of the great contemporary dancers. He engaged her as guest artist with his company and choreographed a new version of *Spectre de la Rose* for her. Judi flew over to Europe to learn the ballet, and I joined her a few times to watch rehearsals. But I felt something was not quite right.

I did not approve of Judi's costume for *Spectre;* she was dressed in a unitard, covered from neck to toe, and she was not the type for unitards. We had an argument over this, with Judi telling me, "That's what Béjart wants, and that's what the designer wants, so that's what I want. I respect them and I won't complain."

"But Judi, it's no good for you. You don't look right," I said.

"I don't care. If that's what they want, that is what I will wear."

I tried to explain to the designer how I felt. The designer wouldn't change a thing, and when I complained further I was promised that the costume would be revised by Béjart when the ballet came to America.

I asked a lot of money for Judi to dance, and Béjart could not afford to have her dance all that often. Though she was expensive, when Judi danced, their performances sold out. And so it was in the United States.

I came to Judi's opening night performance in New York at the Brooklyn Academy of Music, and as usual I went backstage to see her in her dressing room. I also performed my usual ritual: I spat three times at her back, kicked her in the ass, and then said "*merde, merde, merde.*" It's an old custom for artists when they go onstage. I never miss it because I'm superstitious. (Speaking of superstitious, Nora Kaye used to get hysterical if anyone whistled in the theater, and my favorite: Anton Dolin used to tuck a lucky rabbit's foot into his dance belt before he went onstage).

When Judi put on her costume, I almost passed out, because there she was, standing in that awful-looking unitard. It was even worse than what I saw in Paris.

"You cannot go out in this Judi. Impossible," I said.

"What do you want me to do?" she asked.

"You can't go out looking like that." Time was short before she had to be on stage. I went to her makeup table, grabbed a lipstick and an eyebrow pencil, and began to draw lines the length of Judi's body on the unitard, to give it shape and contour. There I was, five minutes before she was to go on stage, redesigning her costume.

"What are you doing?" she asked.

"What the designer should have done," I said. "Now you can go out." And off she went.

It wasn't great, but it looked better than the original.

The ballet was not very well received, though Judi was praised for her performance. But if the public did not care for the ballet, I had to agree with them. I also got the feeling, as did Béjart, that the New York critics did not care for his choreography.

The Universal Ballet

The Universal Ballet is a classical ballet company from Seoul, South Korea, under the direction of Julia Moon. Oleg Vinogradov, who was artistic director of the Kirov Ballet for twenty-five years, has now for several years been artistic director of the Universal Ballet. Julia Moon is related to Reverend Moon. When I saw her the first time I was amazed at what a perfect classical ballerina she is. Even in England, where critics are tough, they considered her a major Giselle. She is a great artist and a wonderful personality onstage. Certain roles requiring bravura technique she should not attempt, but it's not necessary for all great ballerinas to have such a technique.

When Universal Ballet first came to me three years ago, I wanted nothing to do with a company that has support from a religious group. But later on when I saw the company in New York, they were being presented by other agencies in the United States that didn't share my scruples about ballet with religious sponsorship. I thought to myself: it's silly, they are right, why not? And now I realize no one really cares that the Universal Ballet is backed by a church. And not by a church alone, because they have other sponsors—the government of South Korean and some big businesses among them.

The Universal Ballet performs a ballet based on a Korean fairy tale called *Shim Chung*, "The Blind Man's Daughter." The story is based on folklore, and the ballet, stylized and yet authentic, has enjoyed great success with the public. Wherever this ballet, with its extraordinary staging, is presented, audiences can see and learn about the rich cultural heritage of Korea. I'm hoping that the company will continue to represent the rich traditions of Korea's past, while also dancing the classical ballet repertoire.

Whenever I'm interviewed by the press regarding the Universal Ballet, the matter of the Unification Church's involvement is always the first question asked, and I always answer that theater can be separate from, can have nothing to do with religion. I also tell the interviewers, "Look, I think it is absolutely fantastic that a church is helping a ballet company. If you see who helps dance and the other arts, you find Mercedes, Philip Morris, Chase Manhattan Bank, so why not the Moonies?"

America and the Arts

I just cannot believe how people in the present American government seem to have absolutely no sense or feeling for any kind of art. It's as if they find art unnecessary. It's extremely shocking and leads me to wonder how they grew up. What are their backgrounds? How can they be diplomats or officials when they are so ignorant of the arts? This attitude does not exist in other countries. Also, I personally know of a recent American ambassador to France who had to learn French, which until quite recently was the diplomat's international language. I am not a foreign service officer, yet I'm fluent in English, Hungarian, French, and German.

In Europe, it's always been the policy and the custom for governments to help the arts. Not only the governments of today, but the royalty and nobility of the past. Look at Haydn and Count Esterházy! Painters and composers were supported by kings and queens, counts and countesses. When I go abroad, I find people in other countries either can't understand the American government's attitude toward art or are shocked by it. Sure, when some foreign governments give money to support the arts they impose restrictions on its use. They are indifferent to the freedoms we enjoy. But if there is little or no public money available, where does that leave the arts in our country? With Senator Helms and the Bush administration thinking art is hillbilly guitars. When our government has so much money, what does it matter if another hundred million dollars goes to the National Endowment for the Arts?

Henri Matisse

In Paris, at night, I used to walk along the Left Bank of the Seine. I remember being in my forties and thinking about my life, and wanting to get back to those early feelings I had when I first started dancing. It was mostly solitary there by the water, but I saw the Louvre lit up so beautifully that I decided to go back to the museum the following day. It was there that I saw paintings by Henri Matisse and was absolutely taken by him and his vision. I felt the dance in his designs and decided that I must meet him. As I was going to the Riviera, I thought this was a good time to pay him a visit.

I went to Rosella Hightower's ballet school in Cannes, and she told me where Matisse lived and how I could get in touch with him in Vence. I called his apartment, and explained to the lady that answered that I was a ballet dancer and a great admirer of Matisse and that I'd love to meet the master. She said that she would ask him if he was willing to see me. "Call me back tomorrow," she said. When I did, my appointment was set.

Arriving at his home, I was escorted into the bedroom, where Matisse lay in bed, working. He was very friendly and let me see the collages he had all over the walls and ceiling. The colors were gorgeous, in shapes like enormous bird wings. You had the feeling you were not in an ordinary room, but had entered an extraordinary world.

During our conversation, Matisse mentioned the times he designed costumes and scenery for the ballet, and how much he liked dancing and dancers. Matisse did the costumes and decor in 1920 for *Le Chant du Rossignol* for Diaghilev's Ballets Russes. After a short while, I felt it was time to leave. He asked the woman to bring a little book of his designs and he gave it to me as a souvenir. He inscribed it, "Homage à Paul Szilard, Henri Matisse." It's still one of my most cherished possessions.

Before I left, I asked him, "When are you coming to America?" (Of course, we spoke in French). He looked at me and said, "Why should I come to America? There's no light . . ."

We shook hands and I left clutching the book in my hand.

That night, with the meeting with Matisse still fresh in my mind, I walked by the seaside in Cannes. Suddenly, I was thinking of the future: "What will happen when I stop dancing?"

I realized that there were a lot of things one could do in the dance world, even without doing entrechats. Upon returning to New York, I decided that I would organize, produce . . . and why not become an impresario?

INDEX

HOWARD KAPLAN has collaborated on books with Judith Jamison and with Peter Martins, ballet master-in-chief of New York City Ballet. His work has also been included in the Oxford University Press *International Encyclopedia of Dance*. In addition, his children's book, *Waiting to Sing*, was published in 2000. Mr. Kaplan has received fellowships from the MacDowell Colony, the Edward Albee Foundation, and the Bread Loaf Writers' Conference. He currently lives in Washington, D.C.